Executive Jobs Unlimited

Executive

Jobs Unlimited

UPDATED EDITION

by CARL R. BOLL

MACMILLAN PUBLISHING CO., INC.
NEW YORK

COLLIER MACMILLAN PUBLISHERS
LONDON

Library of Congress Cataloging in Publication
Data

Boll, Carl R
    Executive jobs unlimited.

    1. Applications for positions.
    2. Executives.
I. Title.
HF5383.B55 1979   650'.14'024658   79-22953
ISBN 0-02-512790-X

First Printing of Updated Edition 1979
10   9   8   7   6   5   4   3
Macmillan Publishing Co., Inc.
866 Third Avenue, New York, N.Y. 10022
Collier Macmillan Canada, Ltd.
Printed in the United States of America

To the memory of
MR. AND MRS. LOWELL E. JEPSON
of Minneapolis, Minnesota
who urged me to come to America
who gave me both a home and their love
who spurred me on to further education and
who set me an example of service to others

Contents

Foreword, by Donald K. David   ix

Preface   xiii

Preface to First Edition, by Edmond F. Wright   xv

1 The Hard Road—or the Easy One   1

2 The Résumé—Your Stock in Trade   13

3 The Broadcast Letter   33

4 How to Get Interviews Through Advertisers   62

5 Placing Job-Wanted Advertisements   79

6 How to Conduct the Interview   86

7 *Looking for a Job in Secret*   110

8 *From Government to Industry*   119

9 *Executive Search Firms and Employment Agencies*   141

10 *Life Can Begin for You at Fifty—or Sixty—or . . .*   154

11 *For Women Only*   170

12 *When You Are Back on the Payroll*   186

Foreword

I HAVE BEEN ASKED TO WRITE a foreword to this book, which has grown out of the case histories of thousands of people—both old and young, of all races, colors, and creeds—whom the author, Carl Boll, has placed in jobs. Many of these jobs are paying high salaries. This is all the more remarkable when you consider that Carl Boll is not connected with an employment agency but operates his own insurance company, Carl R. Boll & Co., in New York City. He is also an officer and director of a number of manufacturing companies. However, through the years he has proved to be one of those persons who believes in helping his fellow men.

Carl Boll is peculiarly well fitted to counsel people on getting jobs, for he has had an extraordinary variety of work experience himself. Consequently, he has a thorough insight into almost every kind of business. He began earning a living at twelve, then worked successively on ocean liners, farms, in iron mines, factories, department stores, and restaurants. In spite of having to go to work before most boys have entered high school, Carl knew that if he wanted to succeed in life he must first have an education. The tuition for this was not handed to him by a rich father. He had to work for it. As a door-to-door salesman he earned his way through college and graduate school.

After finishing at Carleton College, Northfield, Minnesota, he went on to graduate from the Harvard Graduate School of Business Administration. He was president of its New York Alumni Club during the depression of the 1930's. It was at that time that he started to help the many hundreds who were suddenly thrown out of work. Out of this grew the placement workshop which came to be known as the Thursday Night Club.* This guidance group, which operated without charge, continued to meet in his office for forty years. Thousands of executives have benefited from his sage advice.

Mr. Boll denies that he gets jobs for people, claiming that each man must get his own. However, his tactful yet honest criticism has helped hundreds of men to appraise themselves and their abilities, and so enable them to "sell" themselves to others. For this he has never accepted a fee of any kind. As Mr. Boll says, "Being unemployed is punishment enough without imposing a fine." He believes in teaching each man to help himself so that he never again need fear the specter of being without a job. Once the techniques outlined in this book are mastered, they can always be applied to getting good-paying jobs. These methods work as well in times of depression as they do in times of prosperity.

*Limited to graduates of Harvard Business School.

Carl Boll has written many articles on placement for the *Harvard Business School Alumni Bulletin*. A selection of these articles was compiled in a pamphlet, *Finding Your Job*, which was given out by the Alumni Placement Office. Extracts from this pamphlet have been widely copied by other schools. For instance, Notre Dame University mails a one-page excerpt to every alumnus applying to its placement bureau.

Mr. Boll was chairman of The Committee of One Thousand, which, after the Second World War, helped more than six thousand uniformed men get back into civilian employment.

The New York Alumni of the Harvard Business School expressed their appreciation of the altruistic work of Carl Boll by presenting him with a hand-illuminated scroll. Later, the National Alumni Organization gave him an additional citation for his aid to its graduates. On June 2, 1963, he was given the coveted Alumni Achievement Award from his alma mater, Carleton College.

On April 7, 1964, over five hundred people gathered at Huntington Hartford's Gallery of Modern Art in New York to pay tribute to him. The inscription on the handsome silver tray which was given to him at this time reads, "Carl R. Boll, in appreciation of twenty-five years of devoted and outstanding service—the Harvard Business School Club of New York." As he accepted this tribute to his unselfish work, Carl Boll said, "Twenty-five years seems like a long time. When you multiply this by the fifty-two weeks in a year you get more than a thousand nights that we have worked together to get jobs for those who didn't have them. As I look back on them, they remind me of *The Arabian Nights* or *The Thousand and One Nights*. Our nights together have revealed the depths of each man's troubles, his uncertainties and his heart-aches, and then a miracle—a job."

There are many people holding high positions today who got their jobs by using the methods described by Carl in this book.

DONALD K. DAVID

Dean, Harvard Graduate School
of Business Administration
(1942–1955)
Formerly Director of Ford Motor Co.
Formerly a trustee of the Rockefeller Institute

Preface

SINCE THIS BOOK WAS FIRST PUBLISHED in 1965, the whole business picture has changed. At that time it was taken for granted that the boss or superior was male. Now there are many women in those positions and more are moving up quickly.

Though I recognize that many bosses and interviewers are female, I have chosen to refer to them as masculine rather than use the awkward constructions *he/she* and *man/woman*.

Since women are now being less discriminated against in the business world and since there are new laws protecting them against sex discrimination, there are thousands of them in executive positions.

In spite of their advances and increased opportunities, women still have special problems in the working world. In this new edition I address some of these problems and attempt to help women resolve them.

CARL R. BOLL

xiii

Preface to First Edition

HAVE YOU JUST LOST YOUR POSITION as the result of a merger?
Are you in a "dead end" job? Are you looking for a position
where the pay is better and there is more chance for advancement? Here is a book that will help you get out of the rut of
despair and frustration and well on the road to a more successful and rewarding life. The author, Carl Boll, has helped
thousands to secure jobs—all types of jobs—from office boys
to presidents of some of the largest corporations in America.
His methods have been tested and found successful in thousands of cases during the past twenty-five years. He has
helped others—he can help *you*—if you will only follow the
step-by-step procedures outlined in this book.

Sayville R. Davis, editor of *The Christian Science Monitor*,
said in a speech at the Harvard Business School, "Out of the

hundreds of books written about business, practically none are written by businessmen." They are written by writers. Few businessmen are writers. Of the many books written on job-getting, hardly any, if any, have been by hard-headed businessmen, by men who have tasted the bitter cup of unemployment, or by men who have suddenly found themselves boxed in and up against a stone wall in their jobs. There are dozens of ways by which men have secured jobs. It is ridiculous to attempt to cover all the ways; to do so is to lead the already confused and stunned job-seeker down one alley after another. He goes to friends, counselors, recruiters, employment agencies, etc., until he is exhausted, his morale is gone, and his bank account has been needlessly sacrificed.

There is no book which gives the job-seeker such simple, practical, common-sense direction. There is no other book that gives the job-seeker the fundamental appreciation that every business, in order to succeed, must make a profit; that every employee is necessarily a part of that profit team. No other book shows the job-seeker how he can get this message over to his next employer.

There is no other book which recognizes the fact that an unemployed person is considered a surplus commodity in the job-market, and that it is only by his own effort that he can make himself into a demand product. Surplus products sell at a discount—demand products sell at a premium. No man needs to peddle himself as a surplus, when he can sell himself as "*one of a kind*" and as "*the one man in a hundred*."

There is no other book which shows an unemployed man how to handle the interview, so that *he* is the interviewer, instead of the interviewed. This book shows him how to take the tension out of the interview, thus changing it from a dreaded adventure into a joyful experience. By following these directions, every interview can become a thrilling and profitable undertaking.

There is no other book which shows, beyond the shadow of a doubt, that sometimes the résumé can be more of a hindrance than a help to a job-seeker. This book advises a man never to mail a résumé with a covering letter, nor to take it with him to an interview.

There is no other book which shows a man how to conduct a *sub-rosa* job campaign when he dare not let his employer know that he is looking around for something more rewarding.

There is no other book which teaches a man how to get 20 to 30 per cent interview requests from "Help Wanted" advertisements.

This book contains all the essential ingredients gleaned from hundreds of actual cases. This book, therefore, enables the jobless to avoid many trials and errors on their way from despair to employment. From these cases, there finally evolved a pattern—a pattern which hundreds of men and women have since used with phenomenal success. This book contains no pedagogic rehash from library shelves; everything in it comes from real life experiences. Hundreds of men and women have contributed their know-how to bring this book to you. Each of these people achieved victory from doggedly digging the ingredients out of their past experience. No one can conduct a job-campaign for another. Only *you* can give it strength and plausibility; and it, in turn, will give you confidence.

You now have all the directions you need to chart one of the most exciting and most valuable voyages of your life.

Happy sailing! You are on your way to a more rewarding job!

EDMOND F. WRIGHT

Formerly Director of Placement,
Harvard Graduate School of Business Administration

Acknowledgments

I WISH TO EXPRESS my great appreciation:

To the hundreds of men who so generously let me draw on their letters, résumés and experiences.

To Mr. J. Kendrick Noble of the Noble & Noble Publishing Company for his helpful encouragement at a time when I most needed it.

To my devoted wife Margaret without whose help and nagging this book would never have been finished.

Executive Jobs Unlimited

CHAPTER 1

The Hard Road—or the Easy One

SOMETIMES, a lifeguard, in order to save a person from drowning, stops the victim's frantic splashing and churning about in all directions by knocking him unconscious with a hard punch in the jaw. This enables him to pull the victim back to shore safely. Many people out of a job act much like a drowning man, striking out blindly in all directions, without sense or forethought. I have often wished I could deliver a knockout blow, and with one swift punch drive all the accumulated job-hunting nonsense and trivia out of their heads.

Many people out of a job assume that they know exactly the best and easy way to go about getting one, without giving the matter much thought. They go to employment agencies and executive recruiters. They talk to their business associates, friends, and lawyers. They insert advertisements. They then think that their prayers will be answered. They rush to people who advertise expert job-securing services. Only last week someone showed me a résumé prepared with the help of one of these outfits, which had cost him six hundred dollars. He had proudly mailed it out, but had received not even one job offer for his pains. I have often envied the lifeguard who can shout loudly and clearly, "Stop! Calm down! Use your efforts where they will do the most good!"

Finding a job, or changing one job for another, is a very specialized technique, and I could never understand how a person, completely inexperienced in this field, could assume that he knew a single thing about it. This is too often the case, and it makes it infinitely harder to help him. Sometimes it takes a great deal of energy to persuade a job-seeker to forget the hocus-pocus, and the trite, or the tricky approach. Recently I came across the following clipping about a man who enclosed with his letter a small envelope containing a spoonful of sugar, hoping to sweeten the reception of his letter.

JOB-HUNTER BAITS TRAP WITH SUGAR

Chicago, Aug. 25 (AP)—Fred L. Marx of suburban Deerfield believes in the novel approach in job hunting. He sent out 100 letters to presidents of Chicago companies, each containing a spoonful of sugar done up in cellophane. The letters say that his wife believes he is slightly crazy, but that he frankly hopes the gift will get him a five-minute interview.

Don't waste your time on gimmicks—you can never go wrong being conservative. There is no one so prone to take advice from one and all as a person who is job-hunting. Every time he gets new advice, he changes his approach and strategy; and just as often he changes his course—goes off the main road, and loses both momentum and time. There is, of course, no reason why you should be reading this book and taking the advice that I am trying to give you. There have been others who did not take it, at first.

I well remember one very bright young man, Robert O., who came back to my office after remaining away a long time and said, "I have wasted several months, and it has cost me nearly five thousand dollars in expenses and lost earnings to prove that I was wrong and you were right in your job-getting advice." From then on, he became one of the greatest boosters of my approach to job-hunting.

Realize in Advance That Job-Hunting Is a Hard Task

Job-hunting can become a long, dreary, and lonesome road for the person trying to find a job. One of the best articles written on this subject appeared in an issue of *Fortune* magazine. The title of it was "How Executives Get Jobs," written by Perrin Stryker. I quote: "Whatever their reasons, nearly all executives anxious to change jobs can expect to find the process a lonely, miserable experience. Indeed, finding a new job is about the most difficult, embarrassing, and patience-exhausting venture an executive can undertake." One of the biggest reasons for this is that—and again I quote from the same article—"Top executives are just as stupid about selling themselves as youngsters trying for their first job." It has been my experience that most executives are hog-tied by inhibition, convention, and fear of what the neighbors and former associates might think.

Printers' Ink of November, 1962, published an article called "Job Hunter: the Diary of a Lost Year." I suggest that you read it, as it presents such a vivid picture of one man's experience. It is written from the depths of his scarred soul. He

leads you through his travail, month by month. He had eight
weeks before he lost the use of his office, secretary, and telephone. Thereafter, the telephone booth became his office and
headquarters. His blood really chilled when he had to register
for unemployment compensation and he realized with re-
newed shock that he was a member of the "Unemployed
Society." I quote: "Sixth month: this is where the pavement
really begins to hurt under your feet; where you run down *all*
the leads; where you write to blind box numbers and get no
reply; where you tramp around employment agencies and sit
there with teen-age 'gal Fridays' waiting to be processed;
where you ride sooty little trains across the miasmic marshes
of New Jersey to factories beside smoking slag heaps; where
you rise and shave and stuff your brief case full of résumés
and take the train to nowhere. And, I might add, the commut-
ing to nowhere costs just as much as the ticket to a paycheck,
but you hand it over anyway because today might be *the
day*."

When faced with filling out application forms, he says,
"Some demand information rarely given to anyone outside
our immediate family. Human dignity, I have discovered, is
something more than a four-color spread of a sunset and a
quote from John Stuart Mill. Its essential element is privacy
of your home, your affairs, and your person; that privacy
which permits the little legends which help us live with each
other. But the list (check one) allows no little legends; it
opens up your soul like the front of a doll's house."

After taking psychological and "personality" tests, he says,
"I'm afraid they'll kill an opening I'm qualified for and almost
as afraid they'll get me hired for the wrong reasons. Also, on a
couple of occasions, I've had to take them before I was per-

mitted to talk to anyone, only to find the job was completely outside my area. Two more precious days shot."

I have quoted at length from the *Printers' Ink* article because I wanted you to share the experience of this man so you might get an idea of the possible long and painful road that may lie ahead of you if you take the wrong turn. To show you that the above is not unusual, here are two paragraphs from a letter I received today:

In the past five months I sent out 367 résumés in a direct mail campaign with a 42% reply and 3 interviews, answered 99 advertisements with one interview, registered with seven employment agencies with 1 interview, and registered with all executive recruiters with no interviews. One of the five interviews progressed to the point where the VP wanted to hire me but he was overruled by the President who favored maintaining the status quo until after their peak season.

I would appreciate being allowed to attend your "Thursday Night Club" or any other counseling sessions where I might find what is wrong with my present program and find new and more productive methods of job-hunting.

If you think that these experiences are exceptions, let me give you a jolt and tell you that I have known of hundreds of job-getting experiences that are worse. I have had men come in to see me who have been out of a job for two years and more. In most of these cases, after working with my group for only a few weeks, they were trying to find not just a job but a *better one;* a job not only with more money but with a *better title.* I would like to save you as much time, money, and heartache as is possible by starting you off immediately on the right track and keeping you on it.

Moves You Should Not Make

Like the lifeguard, I would like to stop you from floundering in all directions. These are the immediate moves you should *not* make:

1. Do *not* run at once to your friends and business associates, or big-name contacts. You can see them later when you are ready for them.
2. Do *not* place an advertisement in the job-wanted columns of your favorite paper or trade magazine. In fact, do not place *any* ad until you have studied more productive ways.
3. Do *not* rush to management consultants, executive recruiters, to the so-called head-hunters. They prefer to come to you; you have no glamour for them when you are an unemployed person.
4. Do *not* go to the professional résumé writers. Only *you* can write your résumé; it must come out of your own personal experience.
5. Steer clear of the advice of people who claim that they can get you a job, unless you can afford to waste several hundred or several thousand dollars for their services.
6. Do *not* go away on a vacation, no matter how morbid you feel. The best therapy consists of getting busy on your job campaign and coming to grips with your personal problems. I have yet to find a man or woman who did not later regret having taken a vacation. You cannot help but lose momentum.
7. Do *not* dwell on the politics or frictions that caused you to leave your last job. Get them completely out of your mind, or they will interfere with your concentrating on this exciting new venture.
8. Beware of the "Tin Cup" or the "Brother, can you spare a

dime" approach. Do *not* go to your friends and ask if they know of a job lead. Do *not* go from employer to employer asking if he has an opening.

9. Do *not* contemplate a job change out of your present specialty unless you are prepared to take a lower salary or face the possibility of being out of a job much longer. The greener pasture is too often a mirage—when you get to it, you will find it has the same problems and troubles. Use the very special experience of your present job and apply it to get into a new industry or company. You can work toward a higher position, or in a different direction, when you are *in* the new job; *that* is the time to take every opportunity to take on more responsibility whenever it is available, especially when you are given a chance to broaden or change your direction. It is much easier to sell your past experience because with it you have definite acceptance.

10. Do *not* get caught in the vicious circle of courtesy interviews through the kindness of friends. No one wants to be unkind to a person looking for work, so you will hear, "Sorry, we haven't a thing right now; if you had only come a month ago we could have made a place for you; but I will give you letters of introduction to friends of mine who might use you." This will often embark you on a merry-go-round. I know of one man who was given five letters of introduction by an officer of a large bank. This man kept a record of his interviews. His first contact snowballed into more than a hundred courtesy interviews. Each person wanted either to be helpful or to get rid of the man, and so passed him on happily to the next. Of course, nothing came of any of the interviews, and the man suffered both in loss of time and in loss of morale.

11. Use the third-party approach with great discretion. Often an influential friend or an agency will suggest that they write a letter about you. Your name is not mentioned, but

you are described in the third person. This third-person approach is often both costly and unproductive.

How Then Should You Start?

When I show job-hunters examples of the things others have done in job campaigns, I invariably get the reaction, "Oh, that may be all right for him, but, you see, *I* am different. *I* could not do anything like that." My answer has been the same, thousands of times: "Sure, you are different— thank God you are—and if you weren't, we might all be gunning for the same job. If you were not different, your future employer could simply put all the names of the applicants in a hat, have a grand drawing, and the person whose name was drawn first would get the job. This would be much simpler than trying to cull one out of a hundred—or even a thousand."

I was recently told by one of my men that he knew of a case where there were sixteen hundred applicants who applied for a fairly high-level job in response to an advertisement. Only ten were selected to be interviewed. This dwindled down to three. The man who was chosen got the job because he *was* different from all the rest.

You too can be different; indeed, you must be different. You must make yourself into the one person in a hundred— you can even be the one person in a thousand. You can do this providing you use plain common sense and follow the instructions outlined in the following chapters.

Make Your Job Campaign a Full-Time Job

Do not make unnecessary hurdles for yourself; do not listen to every Tom, Dick, and Harry who is ready with advice and encouragement, which all too often turns into discouragement. They are always eager to tell you what you should, or should not, do. At least one will say, "Why did you ever quit your last job?" or "Didn't you know it is much easier to get a job while you are employed?"

I differ vehemently with this belief. It has been my experience that it is much harder to find or change a job when you are in one. For one reason, it is almost impossible to take out the required time to look for a job when you are working. Holding down a position and conducting a job campaign are each full-time jobs in themselves; neither is done easily or well on a part-time basis.

Exactly how would you go about looking for a job if you were still working? Would you try to sandwich an interview into your lunch hour? Surely you could never have a relaxed interview if you were watching the clock. When would you arrange your interviews—after or during working hours? I am afraid that such maneuvers would affect not only your thinking but your attitude toward your present job as well, and would be very hard to conceal. Furthermore, if your boss found out that you were looking around, you might be asked to resign. It would be foolhardy to expect a promotion or a raise in salary. Then, suppose that you were having an interview in the forenoon or afternoon and the interviewer asked, "Are you employed?" You would have to respond in the affirmative. The next probable questions might be, "Does your employer know that you are looking around? Did he or she give you the time off for this interview?" Obviously, you are now in a dilemma: if you don't have permission, you are stealing the time from your employer, and whatever the answer now is, the brutal fact is obvious—you cannot engender much confidence with the interviewer.

How are you going to look for a job when you are in a job? Do you dare to go to employment agencies, or answer blind newspaper advertisements? Again, you may risk being fired. Do you think that you could possibly do a real job of trying to better yourself when you are inhibited by the fear of "being caught"? Don't let anyone persuade you that you should look for a new job from a firmly entrenched position. After twenty-five years of experience, I find that you are just as acceptable when unemployed. Whether you are employed or not seems to count not at all with prospective employers; they are interested only in what you can do for them.

Do Not Be Dismayed at Minor Discouragements

As you start out on your job campaign you will run into many discouraging interviews. You will be told at various times that you are too old or are too young; that they are looking for a person with more (or less) background and experience. As you study the job descriptions and want ads, you will find that they are looking for a young person, in the middle twenties, who has been to graduate school but who has had from five to ten years of heavy experience. It would be utterly impossible for someone of that age to have had that much experience. You will be told that you are "too big" a person for a certain job and that someone with your valuable experience will have no trouble in making an important connection. You will encounter many more brush-offs. It is hard to understand why employers resort to such flimsy, cruel pretexts. I am of the opinion that they are hiding behind these defensive answers and do not want to tell you the real reason for your turndown.

It is most important that you do not let these things affect your equilibrium or your morale. Realize at the beginning that you are going to get a few knocks, and learn to expect them. You are not going to click with everyone, any more than everyone is going to click with you. You, like most others, will end up with not only one good job but you will probably have several to choose from. This may not be obvious to you in the beginning. The uncertainty of the unknown or of what may be ahead will be your greatest concern.

Let me assure you that you really need not worry. You are embarking on one of the most valuable and exhilarating experiences of your life. Your start of the job campaign is much more important than all the other aspects of your search for a job. That is why I wish I could be like the lifeguard and save you from all the false starts and wasteful motions, the heartaches, and headaches, and embarrassments which follow the wrong initial move. Of equal importance, I would like to save you both time and money. Remember that when your income stops, everything that you or the family do, every telephone call, all correspondence and postage, all transportation costs, come out of your capital funds, your savings, or loans. If you wish to experiment, remember that the cost will come out of your own pocket.

For twenty-five years I have observed hundreds of men and women and have noted the results of their experiences. I have watched them fumble and experiment. Twenty-five years ago I fumbled along with them, and the things I relate in the following chapters are the refinement of methods that have been tried and have been found to work. These are not *theories* on how to get a job; these are *methods that have worked* hundreds and hundreds of times. You can learn to meet an interviewer as an equal and go into the interview with dignity; you do not have to go in with your tail between your legs, or with a tin cup in your hand. Start on the high road and stay out of the "Slough of Despond." Benjamin Franklin once wrote: "Experience keeps a dear school, but fools will learn in no other."

Your First Task

Your very first move is to prepare your résumé.* Stay with it until you feel a glow of satisfaction come over you. I well remember one woman who had tramped the streets for months before she came to see me. After she had fashioned her résumé as I suggested she told me that at last she began walking with her head in the air; for the first time since being out of work she felt that she was somebody. Your résumé should describe you as a useful and saleable commodity. It will take you out of the "unemployed or surplus group" and put you into the "demand or premium product" category. In the market place, it is always the premium product that commands the higher price.

Let us now start to convert you into a product that can beat out the competition. Let us make you so different that you will be that *one person* in a thousand. You are *you;* there is no other person quite like you; you are truly different. Somewhere out there there is an employer who wants and needs *you* and is willing to pay your price. As Stanley Marcus was once told by his father when he started in business, "Remember, there is no piece of merchandise that someone doesn't want." You are now that piece of merchandise.

---

* I use the word "résumé" reluctantly, because it is used so much in the job market and turns out too often to be merely a passive recital of functions which may do more harm than good. When I speak of "résumé," I mean an inventory of your achievements. Read the next chapter on how to accomplish this.

CHAPTER 2

The Résumé-Your Stock in Trade

AT THIS POINT, before you do one other thing, start to work on your résumé. Forsake all other things for the moment. It is absolutely necessary that you prepare a résumé. Without it, you are nothing more than an empty drifting boat, wallowing on the waves. Until you have your experience material fairly well in hand, you are not prepared and should make no attempt to see people. A carelessly prepared résumé will present a poor impression of your value, and you may never be able to overcome the harm it may do.

The Content of the Résumé

The résumé should be an inventory of your past business experience. I like to compare a résumé to a Sears catalog, out of which the proper merchandise (in your case, the appropriate experience) can be pulled out of stock as needed in order to make the sale. Your résumé, then, is your shelf stock—your saleable merchandise. You will not need to use all of it every time you apply for a job. You must, however, develop it so that it includes all the details of your past work experience, so that you can utilize whatever portion of it may be applicable at any given time with reference to any particular job.

The Form of the Résumé

When you start preparing your résumé, don't worry too much about what the final form will be. Content is much more important. So much fuzzy stuff has been written about form, without enough concern about content, that many of the résumés I see are utterly insipid. Most of them fail to consider the viewpoint of the person who is going to hire you; often they lack judgment, common sense, and objectivity. Some people have shown résumés of this kind to me and said, "But I did it according to such and such a book," or, "It must be all right. I worked with a counselor and paid him blank hundred dollars." Let me brief you on what I think is wrong with the general run of résumés that I have reviewed. Most professional résumé writers advise you to prepare a one- or two-page résumé. Generally, you are told to use a standard format. Some tell you to begin with the most intimate details and vital statistics of your life—your age, health, marital status, number of children, height and weight. Some require your social security number, draft status, father's occupation, mother's maiden name, religious and social affiliations, and even family lineage. All of this is based on the false assumption that a person will be hired on the basis of the vital statistics outlined in his printed résumé. In my experience, nothing is farther from the truth. No employer* is initially concerned with these details, even though his company will probably ask for some of them for their records after you have been hired. He does not care whether you came from the wrong side of the tracks, or whether your ancestors arrived here before the Indians. It just might, in some instances, be better if you *did* come from the other side of the tracks. Many of our business leaders are very proud of their humble origins. Neither should you consider physical size, appearance, or impairment a deterrent in getting a job. Do you think anyone ever gave this consideration at General Electric when Steinmetz was hired? None of these things really matters to an employer. The only thing that will truly impress him is the answer to "What have you done?" "What have you accomplished in your other jobs?" You will be compared and weighed in the scales against others on the basis of your past *performance*, and your *accomplishments*.

Business Exists to Make a Profit

At this point, I want to digress to be certain that when you tabulate your accomplishments you head in the right direction. You must realize that business exists for one purpose only, and that purpose is *to make a profit*. This profit must be large enough to pay and attract top personnel, to attract money from stockholders, institutions, and banks. Business must make sufficient profit to spend on research, better tools and facilities. It must create new and better products in order to stay alive and vigorous in a vicious competitive market.

*Though many employers and interviewers are female today, I have chosen to refer to them as masculine throughout the book to avoid the use of cumbersome constructions such as he/she.

Your Job Does Count

Perhaps you feel that your job is in such a minor capacity that you need pay no attention to the profit motive in business, that it is of no concern to you. In an article, "Jobs Cost Money," Malcolm Forbes states that in the 100 highest-ranking manufacturing companies, an investment of $24,000 per job is required. It averaged $53,000 in the distilling business, and $62,000 in the petroleum industry, to give a man a job. In today's economy, these figures should be doubled. Never forget, no matter how large or how small your position is, that you are counted as a part of this average. Everyone *must* contribute his part to the earnings or profits in order to stay in the work force. This applies even on the farm—a dry cow or an unproductive pig or hen goes to the butcher. You may not be able to measure your share with exactitude; however, your past accomplishments or your work performance should tell whether or not you have contributed to the over-all picture.

You may be in a business where the amount of investment is not obvious, such as an advertising agency, consulting firm, or an accounting firm. The investment, however, is there; someone has put up the costly office building. Your employer in renting space is renting the use of invested capital. He pays dearly for its use. If the business is not making the profits to pay his rent, he is dispossessed. It is not my intention to give you a lesson in economics. I am merely trying to bring home to you a too often forgotten concept about business—namely, that it *must make a profit to exist*. Businesses are so large these days that an individual in a particular company may forget and get a feeling that he may not be important. But, in reality, each person is a part of the profit team.

Why Pick You?

Why does an employer hire you instead of someone else? Is it because your shoes are shined, your pants are well pressed, and your hair is properly combed? These are certainly not his primary considerations or motivations, though if these details have been taken care of, they may be a factor in his judgment. He will ultimately hire you because he thinks you can help him make a profit in his business. He hires you because he hopes you will do more to add to the productivity of his business than some other applicant. Thus, he has the use of one measurement only on which to base his judgment— namely, *your employment record.* It will be up to you to convince him how much your performance contributed to the profit of your previous employers.

Why You Should Be Interested in Profits

Anything that adds to the smooth-running operation of the business, to its more successful operation, also adds to the profit picture. Someone recently asked, "Give me the definition of a successful business," and the answer came quickly: "A profitable business." You must get this concept, this philosophy of profit or performance, into every line of your résumé. Only then will you be talking the language of the person who is interviewing you. If you *can* get this simple common-sense idea into your thinking and hence into your résumé, you will then be the one person in a hundred, or even in a thousand, who is called in and has a chance at a job. You will have made yourself different; you have become a demand product.

How to Get This Profit-Consciousness Across

Your problem now is to get across to your prospect the fact that you are aware of the profit-consciousness necessary in his business. Can you do it by merely listing the number of functions you have performed previously? No. Can you do it by reciting concrete deeds? Yes. Study the following two paragraphs. They were written by the same personnel man:

I carried out an active nation-wide technical recruitment program, involving employment agency contacts, college interviewing, and considerable advertising. This program made possible extensive organizational growth.

There is no zip to this paragraph. This man gives no concrete factual measurements of his performance. He simply states the functions he performed, and these he embellishes with adjectives of self-appraisement, such as "active," "considerable," "extensive." Avoid words of self-evaluation like the plague. The writer tried to show with words how he contributed to the company's success. He gave no measurable results or achievements. Now note this revised version:

I recruited technical personnel.
I sparked laboratory expansion from 90 to 500 men.
I developed new supply sources for technical manpower by interviewing in 50 colleges and universities.
I scoured the country to see men at hotels, colleges, and conventions.
I increased inquiries from 50 to 75 a week by means of advertising.

Do you see the difference? You would never guess that these two paragraphs describe the same man. Concrete, factual statements carry a powerful message and create indelible mental images. Simply mentioning abstract functions does not leave the necessary mental picture. *Measure your deeds.* You must create a mental picture to *make you stand out* from the other applicants.

Oh, Yes: You Can Measure Your Accomplishments

I hear over and over again, "But I can't show measurable results like that man does. My job just wasn't like that." Or "That may be all right for a salesperson who piles up sales, or a budget manager who holds costs in line, but my job was different."

Perhaps I can best convince you by showing you what happened in the case of a public-relations woman who had this point of view. The first of the following résumés is the one she originally brought to me:

Director of Public Relations,———Foundation
I was responsible for over-all planning and execution of Public Relations programs. I disseminated information and promotions for all Foundation projects and publications. I was the liaison for mass media and other agencies having similarly oriented programs in world affairs, particularly the United Nations. I conceived and executed long-range programs. I served as a catalyst for world affairs and peace projects. I prepared releases, brochures, and news bulletins.

When you read the paragraph above, you may well wonder how this can possibly be turned into a list that shows performance or specific deeds accomplished; but when you look at the following rewrite of the above, you can see how it was done:

Director of Public Relations,———Foundation
Directed an anniversary program called, "Perspective of Peace."

I was responsible for 2,000 newspaper free publicity items.

I had eight articles published in national magazines.

Arranged free broadcasts by 21 domestic radio stations and 4 television companies.

Disseminated 20 news stories on a world-wide basis through the U.S. Information Agency.

Secured participation by 600 colleges in *World Affairs* programs.

I persuaded 125 national organizations to stimulate peace programs, including the Y.M.C.A., the League of Women Voters, and the U.S. Chamber of Commerce.

This woman reworked her whole résumé in this style.

In her first letter to me, she wrote, "You have revolutionized my attitude toward job-hunting. I am convinced that what you taught me will greatly improve my effectiveness in finding the job I am looking for."

Her second letter to me, a month later, read, "Believe it or not, my new position is the direct result of the conferences we had together. The résumé you helped me write was actually the vital factor."

Of Course You Are Different

No one can write a résumé that is exactly like another person's, because each person must use his own material. You build your own résumé on the basis of what you have done; hence your own image emerges. If you are a foreman, tell how much better your shift does than that of another foreman. Has your boss commended you for leaving a clean place for the next shift? How does your safety record compare with that of another foreman? How many of your work team quit you in the last year? How many new people have you had to train?

What have you done in your job that makes you proud?

Think about all the things you have done—even the ones that seem small and inconsequential to you. If you saved your firm money, increased sales with fewer clerks, or made a similar accomplishment, you are a wanted person. Get your message across.

This same technique can be applied to all jobs, great or small. It applies to any person who is sincere and wants a higher salary. I said *sincere*, for if you are lazy and a shirker, unwilling to make your place a better place in which you and others work, or unwilling to push so that your boss gets back two dollars for one that he invests in you, then this book is not for you. Just keep on punching a time clock and carrying a chip on your shoulder. There is not, and there should not be, a better job for you.

Examples of Good Résumé Construction

1) General Manager
   I increased aircraft output from 8 to 135 planes a month, in less than one year.
   I reduced the work force from 18,000 to 11,000 in the same period.
   I reduced manpower hours per plane from 17,000 to 8,000.
   I decreased loans from 51 million to 19 million.

If you were the president of a corporation that had been having production and money problems, and this person came to your attention, wouldn't you want to interview him or her? Of course you would; you could not afford to do otherwise.

2) Sales Manager
   Increased sales $350,000 and saved $180,000 in field selling costs.

Reduced field sales force from 80 to 47 people.

Upgraded quality of salespeople through increased compensation.

Reduced turnover from 58 to 3 people a year.

Instituted direct field controls over damaged and shopworn merchandise.

Are you beginning to understand what I mean by concrete examples? This one gives true quantitative measurement. There is no time wasted here in getting the message over; it comes across loud and clear.

3) Director of Administration   Jones & Jones, Inc.
Engineering and Research Development Laboratory

1. Set up policy to make a profit on every Engineering Research and Development contract.
2. Made $700,000 annual engineering profit (previous losses had averaged $100,000).
3. Set up a tenfold engineering manpower expansion in Multi Plant Divisions.
4. Developed a recently acquired subsidiary from a 15-man development shop to a $1,000,000 manufacturing business, and thereby produced a $70,000 profit.
5. Set up centers of profit accountability under project managers.
6. Developed profit and price control without stifling creativity.

These examples show how one can get the story across quickly and sharply. Each person had come to me with a résumé full of abstract functional phrases. In all cases I began by asking them to tell me in their own words what they meant by each statement, what they had actually accomplished. Usually, what people tell you is so much better than what they have written that I ask them to write it in just that way. Over and over again I have to ask them, "But what was the end result?" Often they tell me in narrative form. I then urge them to condense it into sharp and concise statements.

The Format of the Résumé

1. *Words*. Use simple words, monosyllables whenever you can. Langley Carelton Keys, in his article in the January-February issue of the *Harvard Business Review*, defines this problem and gives examples. He brings out clearly the thought I am trying to convey to you. He flays omnibus paragraphs, abstract words, and passive verbs for fouling up communications in business. He cites as an example: "In a large dairy company, a subordinate had written a long two-page memorandum concerning vacations. It was written with plenty of abstract polysyllables for dignity, passive verbs for avoiding responsibility, long sentences for obscurity. He had never used one word when he could use three. As a result, the memorandum was obscure, long-winded, and ineffectual."

Do not use the same word more than once or twice in the same paragraph. It is monotonous and deadly. Employ Roget's *Thesaurus of Words and Phrases* to find other and stronger words with the same meaning.

Use picture-creating words.

2. *Sentences*. Start your first sentences with direct action verbs, such as "directed," "developed," "sparked," "originated," etc. This gives you direct credit for the deed and strengthens the whole fiber of your material. Don't be prudish about using the personal pronoun "I." If you don't take credit, how is the reader going to know about you? Forget the old adage about people coming to your door because you make a better mouse trap. It doesn't happen any

more. It takes from 15 to 20 million dollars in advertising to get even a better toothpaste on the market today.

Keep each sentence down to *ten* or *twelve* words. This means working and reworking it again and again, but it is well worth the effort. It will give your résumé a telegraphic staccato effect that will pull the reader along. Pretend that you have to get your story across in a fifty-word telegram.

3. *Paragraphs.* Keep your paragraphs down to three or four lines. Single space the paragraphs but leave at least a double or triple space between them. This helps to divide each subject and provides the reader with a thought pause to comprehend and digest it.

I believe this telegraphic pattern has had a great deal to do with my success in placing people. I have found that unless the reader can quickly absorb material while he scans through it, you have lost him.

Long complex sentences and lengthy paragraphs leave a blurred image or none at all. Nothing is so frustrating as to have to read a paragraph several times and even then not get the meaning of it.

Be Objective

You must be objective in your thinking. All too often I find résumés full of subjective sentiments. Put yourself in the place of the one who reads your material. What would you want to know about the person you have to hire if you were to sit on the other side of the desk? All through the résumé you must make statements about real accomplishments and the part you played in them. Often I hear a job-seeker say, "But I did this as a team effort; there were many others helping, too." I then ask, "Were you responsible for getting it done? If it had failed, would you or someone else get the blame? If you would get the blame, are you not then justified in taking the credit?"

Crawford H. Greenwalt, president of DuPont, writes about this in his book *The Uncommon Man*. He says, "Authority can and must be delegated, responsibility can never. For even though one officer may delegate to a subordinate full authority for conducting the affairs of a department or an activity, the ultimate responsibility remains his own. No matter how much responsibility we assign to others, our own stands undiminished." Now I hope this clears up any misgivings you may have in taking credit for your accomplishments.

Develop Power in Your Résumé

To develop power in your résumé, first of all, get yourself a copy of one of the management handbooks. There are a number of good ones.

1. *Defining the Manager's Job—the A.M.A. Manual of Positive Descriptions*. Published by the American Management Association.
2. *Top Management Handbook*. Published by McGraw-Hill Inc.
3. *Business Management Handbook*. Published by McGraw-Hill Inc.

It is neither possible nor necessary to give you a list of all the functional handbooks that are published on management. I mention these so you can find a handbook in your job category. This makes it possible for you to list all the possible functions in your field. When you have them listed, then try to write down achievements for as many of them as possible. I have for years referred people to these published by the Ronald Press, New York:

Office Management Handbook
Materials Handling Handbook
Cost Accountant's Handbook
Financial Handbook
Marketing Handbook
Personnel Handbook
Production Handbook

There are others which might contain more relevant material for you. You will find some of them in the business section of public libraries. Get any that are available, for it doesn't make too much difference which you use. They are to be used only as guidelines to help you organize your material. For instance, Prentice-Hall publishes:

Business Methods Handbook
Taxes Handbook

In these handbooks, you will find lists of job categories such as President, General Manager, Treasurer Controller, Sales Manager, etc. Find your job category. Take all of the functions listed and then put one function *only* at the top of each sheet of paper. Just disregard all functions that do not apply to your case.

Now develop each function, putting down exactly what you did and what was accomplished by it. In order to create a concrete picture, measure each deed in terms of figures or percentages. Your résumé is now taking form.

Do not intermingle functions. If you are a financial man, stay in the groove. Do not mention other things that you may have done but which do not relate to a financial position. If you have dabbled in sales, do *not* mention it, for you weaken your position. The world is looking for specialists, so be one, at least until you get the job.

Work this résumé over and over. Set it aside for a day or two. Go back to it. *Think* about it and rewrite it again and again.

Doing a good job on this résumé will greatly add to your self-esteem and give you just the lift you need at this time.

Will the Company Benefit From Hiring You?

Any employer, before he places you on the payroll, wants to be reasonably certain that the investment he puts in you—in time, in overhead, fringe benefits, and salary—is going to yield more than he puts out. He must get this investment back, just as a farmer who plants his seed corn expects a yield far in excess of what he planted. Sure, the farmer gambles—on the elements and on having put his time and capital in land and equipment. It is, however, a calculated risk. If he felt otherwise, he would be better off to feed his seed corn to his pigs.

The operating executive must account to his stockholders as to his being a good servant. He must show a profit in return for the use of both liquid and fixed capital entrusted to him. Your résumé must show that you are profit-conscious. Business is nourished and grows on profits only. It is as dependent upon profits as is a baby on its bottle. Industry, and even service and charitable organizations, need to make ends meet or they become stunted and wither away. It has always seemed strange to me that even high-salaried people, when they write their résumés, overlook this basic profit concept.

If you state in your résumé that you increased sales, ask

yourself, "Were they on a more profitable basis?" Or are you like the man who sold hot dogs? He made them so tasty that people for miles around came to buy. He lost money on every hot dog he sold, but he claimed he made that up in volume.

I will always remember that after a speech by President Lazarus of Federated Stores, someone asked him from the floor, "Haven't your sales fallen off lately?" Mr. Lazarus replied, "Young man, we are not interested in mere sales; we are interested in profits, and they haven't fallen off."

If you are a controller (general manager or financial executive) and state in your résumé that you installed a $50,000 machine accounting system or one of the latest electronic data processing devices costing a million dollars, then ask yourself the questions, "So what? What good did it do? Did it reduce costs? Did it give management reports one day or ten days sooner or even hours sooner? Did it give daily reports? Did it control inventory in line with sales? Did it reduce capital tied up in raw or finished inventory?"

Did your system show where and when to put greater sales effort? Did your system show management the profitable merchandise and suggest discontinuing the unprofitable items?

If you are a financial person, did you plan capital expenditures? Did you point out which activity—profitwise—was most worthy of the use of capital? Did you show the payout period? How did the use of capital compare with your prediction?

Did you manage to reduce the amount of working capital tied up in inventory? I remember one man, a general manager of heavy industrial products, who took over the management when the average inventory was 25 million and sales just over 30 million. Three years later his sales had gone up to 90 million, but his inventory was now only 32 million. Can you imagine the impact that this would make on a future employer? He also increased the inventory turnover three times, and completely eliminated all bank loans. This man is now president of a well-known company. This is what I mean when I tell you: Show that you are profit, money, cost, expense, overhead, and sales-turnover minded. This will make your interview much easier and also make it much easier for you to sell yourself into a job.

I will undoubtedly be criticized by some people for laying so much stress on profits and money. In the minds of some, profit seems to be synonymous with sin. I'll challenge any of these critics to run a business or a service without it, or to meet a payroll without it. Money and profits are not everything; they are, however, the universal medium of exchange and measurement. Money is the lubricating oil which keeps our economy from grinding to a halt. Where there are no profits and there is none expected, investors turn away and seek other opportunities, bankers refuse to lend, suppliers refuse credit, and smoke stops coming out of chimneys. Business must choose between profitable and unprofitable ventures.

I am indebted to Roger Blough, president of the U.S. Steel Corporation, for the following quotation. This is from his recent San Francisco speech on the *Unprofitable Puzzlement:* "What is it that creates tall buildings against the sky, provides jobs for over 65 million Americans, creates laboratories where wonder drugs are born, begets the tools of production, provides industry muscle to resist aggression? It is the most unprofitable thing for a free society to be without. Behind all these, in a free society, is the one great motivating force, the one driving power, and that is the incentive we call PROFIT."

Don'ts for Résumé Use

1. Never mail your résumé with your letter asking for an interview. Many advisors, I know, do advise this, but I can't warn you strongly enough against it. Why should anyone ask you in for an interview when he thinks he already knows all about you—in fact, more than he may want to know? Mailing a résumé to ask for an interview just kills off the possibility of the interview you are striving to get.

2. Do not mail a formal résumé when answering advertisements in newspapers or in trade magazines.

3. Do not mail a résumé, even after a request to do so by a telephone call. By all means *resist* being interviewed over the telephone. Your interview *must* be person to person.

4. Do not mention in a letter that you have prepared a résumé. If you do, you will be asked to mail it in, and that will kill all chances of your getting an interview. I have found that just mentioning you have a résumé cuts your interviews down 75 per cent.

5. Try to do without a résumé when you go into an interview. You may feel that you need it for the first few times—some folks tell me they feel as though they were going in naked without a résumé. Learn to do without this crutch as soon as possible. Only one interviewer in four will insist on it and then you will have to give him something. If it makes you feel any better, stick it in your pocket, but do not bring it out. Interviewing in this way requires that you and the employer look each other in the eye. This way he can gauge your personality, and you can discern the breakthroughs. This will be developed more thoroughly in the chapter on "How to Interview."

6. Do not print your résumé—certainly not at the begin-

ning of a campaign. Doing so freezes and fixes it. Résumés will, and should, grow with your interviews. They will bring out important facts and accomplishments which you may have forgotten or have considered too trivial to mention. When you keep your résumé fluid, you have a chance to develop one specially directed and sharpened to fit the requirements of the positon for which you are interviewed.

One man wrote me that he had had about thirty interviews in his campaign, for which he prepared twelve specially directed résumés. Nearly 95 per cent of the people I have counseled have been in the high-income bracket. Nevertheless, this same method is applicable for anyone—a stenographer, a clerk, a bookkeeper, a foreman.

The Experience of an Office Clerk

When this boy came to me in desperation, he had been out of work for many, many weeks. He had been making the rounds from office to office trying to get a job. Times were tough—there were 7 or 8 million unemployed. This lad could never get past the reception desk. I asked him to make a résumé. This is it. "My working experience is limited. My only job has been with the Associated Willkie Clubs. I was in charge of the mailing department. I ran the multigraph and postage meter machine. I have had one year of college where I was proctor in the dormitory. I was an Eagle Scout, a camp counselor, and then an assistant Scout Leader."

After an hour or two of digging, we came up with this résumé:

Office and Mail Clerk   *Associated Willkie Clubs*
I opened all mail received at headquarters.

I accounted for up to $5,000 in daily cash and check contributions.

I daily accounted for, and distributed, several thousand dollars in U.S. Government postage stamps.

I ran off thousands of copies of letters on the multigraph presses.

I was personally entrusted by Mr. Willkie to carry confidential messages to and from Republican Headquarters.

I kept a crew of 50 to 200 volunteer workers supplied with campaign material for publicity.

We embodied some of these items in a letter to the presidents of fifty companies. We did not mail out the résumé— just the letter. This boy had more job offers than he had ever dreamed possible. Within two weeks, he was working at his new job.

Your résumé will be the basis of one of the most important documents you will ever write. It is worthy of painful efforts. If this résumé is to have any power or strength, it will have to come out of your very soul. The process is going to be painful and difficult. You can't build muscle tone by letting someone else do your setting-up exercises for you; you can't win any races if someone else does the training. You must formulate your résumé yourself. Try to place yourself in the position of the employer and tell him what you would like to know about a future employee if you were in his place.

CHAPTER *3*

The Broadcast Letter

SOME YEARS AGO I wrote an article on job-finding under the title of "Miracles." Today, I still think that nailing down a job as a result of a job campaign is like performing a miracle. Too many people when out of a job expect the impossible. They hope that an employer will seek them out wherever they may be and offer them just the right kind of a job. They want miracles to happen, forgetting that miracles just don't happen —they must be performed. Every miracle I have ever read about has been wrought by someone. If you desire an abundance of bread and butter on your table, you have in your own hands the power to get it there. For over twenty-five years I have watched job-getting miracles unfold before my eyes. Tired, beaten, unbelieving men and women who followed the simple procedures and job philosophy outlined in these pages have worked their own miracles.

33

You Can't Sell From an Empty Wagon

In a previous chapter, I advised you that getting your résumé prepared was of the greatest importance in starting a job campaign. We will assume now that it has been organized. Your résumé is your stock in trade, your saleable merchandise. It becomes the basis of your job campaign. Without it, you would be like the picture that Dun & Bradstreet circulated during the depression. It showed an old country peddler standing beside his empty horse-drawn wagon. Underneath the title was the inscription, "You can't sell from an empty wagon." Your résumé represents the inventory of goods that you put into your wagon.

The whole purpose of everything you do now is to find as many buyers of your services as you can. You may have the most perfect qualifications for a job, but unless you can talk to employers, your qualifications are as useless as a book that lies unread on a library shelf, or as ineffectual as the Fuller Brush man who doesn't get a chance to open his case before a housewife. If you want a better job, you must get interviews, interviews and more interviews.

How to Get Interviews

More than twenty years ago I discovered what every placement person must eventually conclude—that is, that the right individual is never available when you have a job lead; and when you do have the person available, the right job is not at hand. Consequently, when I first started this work and had an office full of people looking for jobs, I had to get them activated. They branched out in every direction. They called on all possible employment agencies. They used letters of introduction. They answered advertisements, and they inserted "Job Wanted" ads themselves.

At one time, as placement chairman of an alumni association, in order to get leads, I mailed out 15,000 letters countrywide. I enclosed a self-addressed return card, on which I requested employers to list job leads. Hundreds of leads came in, but there were very few that fitted the abilities of my people or resulted in anyone's getting a job. The big thing I learned, from all this indiscriminate prospecting, was that job leads are, as a rule, for very specific persons with specific experiences. Even though one is constantly told that the business world desires people with broad backgrounds, it nonetheless wants individuals with specific experience. The business world calls for specialists.

Some of the job-seekers got friends to write a letter about them to prospective employers. Here is an example from one such letter: "I know of a man who has fine qualifications as a sales manager. He is an excellent man of proven character, and I will gladly arrange for you to see him," etc. I do not recommend this approach. The results of third-party letters are very poor and very disappointing. I remember one man for whom an agency mailed out 350 letters to firms on a list he bought from it (the agency is paid a commission if a job is secured through it). He received only one interview, but no job. I regard third-party letters as the least successful of all approaches. I don't advise using it unless the job-seeker has to work on a *sub-rosa* basis.

Value of the Broadcast Letter

After trying one method after another to secure interviews, the experience of several of my job-seekers opened my eyes to a new avenue, and I began to realize the value of mailing out "broadcast" letters written in the first person.

One man had been making the rounds seeing company officers with letters of introduction furnished by two influential business friends. He had no trouble at all in getting in for a courtesy interview, but none of these interviews resulted in a single job offer.

When he had exhausted his list, his energy, and his morale, I persuaded him to write a letter directly to the presidents of several hundred companies. He picked the names from a directory. The list included a goodly number of the presidents of companies he had previously seen. To my great surprise, he received replies from half of those to whom he had written, and 5 per cent of these suggested he call for an interview. One of these came from a president he had seen just two weeks earlier. When he had been interviewed on the basis of his letter of introduction, he had been told that there was no job available. However, when that same president received his personal broadcast letter, he wrote that he had turned it over to his vice-president in charge of manufacturing and suggested that the applicant arrange an appointment with him. The man followed through, had his interview, was hired, and is still with this same company—twenty years later.

This broadcast letter incident opened my eyes to the potential use of this approach and taught me that the letter does something that nothing else seems to do. Its message penetrates right into the inner office. The letter short-circuits not only lesser officers and impersonal personnel departments but frequently makes it possible to get to see the president or another officer of the firm. As a result of this kind of letter, when you are invited for an interview, you do not have to fight your way past a protective secretary who is adamantly trying to see that her boss is not disturbed by a job-seeker. Your letter will have done the preparatory job for you unlike anything else. It will have put the focus on the exact position you want, and now that you have been invited in, you are on an entirely different footing: you come in as a peer.

This is a letter I received from one of the men who, reluctantly but at my insistence, sent out some broadcast letters:

DEAR CARL,
I'm sorry that I can't be with you on Thursday night. I have an interview out of town. In fact, I have eight more interviews lined up ahead. I sent out 225 letters. They just exploded into interviews. My coat tails have been standing out straight ever since the mailing. I'll report to you as soon as something is definite.

He landed a job as general manager of a machine shop in New Jersey employing 2,000 men. A miracle? Yes. One wrought by a human being such as you, but one who had faith and energy enough to make this effort. Today, over 90 per cent of all the people I work with find their jobs and are placed through the broadcast-letter campaign. These letters are sent out *cold* to unknown presidents of companies which the applicant did not even know existed until he found their names in a directory. Therefore, your most important task is to get your broadcast letter out at once.

It doesn't make any difference whether you are looking for a job that pays $5,000 or $50,000. Get those broadcast letters in the mail. Of all the methods of job-finding I have had people try, I have found the broadcast letter the most positive, the most effective, the most time-saving, and the most reasonable way to get placed. Do not be persuaded otherwise. This does not mean that jobs cannot be located by other means. I have always told people that they should use every possible means available to get placed. In other words, shake every tree and turn over every stone; but before exploiting other avenues, get those letters in the mail. I speak from long experience. Many individuals who tried other means first belatedly and sadly turned back to the broadcast letter.

After your broadcast letters have been mailed, you can generally count on from ten to fifteen days of comparatively free time. The first answers you will receive will be the "no" answers. These will come in immediately. You will then get courtesy replies from presidents stating they haven't a job for someone as good as you but assuring you that anyone of your stature should have no trouble finding a place. This is plain baloney.

The next letters that come in will contain application blanks for you to fill out. These will be from personnel departments and should arrive a few days after you have made your mailing. The letters suggesting you call for an interview lag and come in later. Usually, they reach their peak about the eighth or tenth day after mailing, and then they begin to level off. So, during the first week before you get your requests for interviews, you can hit the town, visit your friends, see employment agencies, and follow any leads you may have. After the tenth day, as a result of your broadcast letters, you should have plenty of appointments ahead.

Keep Them Going Out

There is a great difference between the interviews that result from the broadcast letter and those otherwise obtained. Time and again I have been told that interviews resulting from letters are infinitely superior. *Keep mailing out broadcast letters*. Get out a hundred or two each week. Keep mailing them out, even though you feel fairly certain after a particular interview that you "have it made" and that the offer of a job is only minutes away.

Sometimes jobs are like mirages—they fade away. I strongly advise you to get out another hundred letters even when you feel you have a job cinched. Nothing is so depressing and demoralizing as to find that the job you counted on has fallen through and you don't have any more interviews scheduled ahead. I have known this to happen many times. Profit by this experience and don't insist on learning it the hard way. Keep the broadcast letters going out. Should they result in several job offers, you have a choice. One of the greatest boosts to your morale is to be in a position to turn down a job; it gives you a wonderful feeling of security.

Over the years, the average number of interviews per 100 letters sent out by people I have coached runs to about 6 per cent. It probably will run double that amount and even go higher for jobs in the medium and lower echelons. After all, if you want to be a general manager, remember that there is only one job in that category in a given company. There can be only one controller, whereas there may be a half-dozen regional sales managers, several hundred salesmen, and so on. It is like the Army—one general, several colonels, more captains, then a greater number of lieutenants and sergeants. Because there are necessarily fewer job-openings in the higher echelons, you must get out a much larger mailing.

The Physical Aspect of Your Letter

You need not go to the expense of having each letter individually written. Individual letters are more expensive to get out, and the results are no better than those gained from letters that are mechanically reproduced. Reproduced letters cost one-quarter to one-third of the price of individually written ones. Do not let anyone persuade you that it is necessary to use individually typed or individually reproduced letters unless the cost is of no account to you. Cost *is* important to most job-seekers. Have your letters multilithed, or use any process which prints through a ribbon so that, except for experts, the typing cannot be distinguished from that which is individually done. It is very important, moreover, that you match the ink and type of the body of the letter when you fill in the names and addresses.

An inexpensive way to print your broadcast letter is to use the photo-offset process. An ingenious method of using photo-offset from a cost-conscious job-seeker is summarized below:

1. Change the standard ribbon in your typewriter to an I.B.M. carbon ribbon. Though this is a messy job, the new ribbon will yield a bold dark imprint that is similar to the imprint made by your own typewriter when you put in a new standard black ribbon.

2. Leaving blank spaces for the date, name, address, and salutation, type the letter carefully. I advise against using letterhead. You do not want to call so much attention to your name in case you want to write another letter. Just type your address in the upper left-hand corner, and your telephone number in the lower left-hand corner.

3. Have the letter photo-offset.

4. Change the ribbon in your typewriter to a new standard black ribbon. Simply type in the dates, names, addresses, and salutations as needed, and sign each letter. The type should match the offset-printed letter, giving the impression of an individually typed letter. You can do as many or as few as you wish each day.

If you prefer, get a price breakdown from a letter-mailing service for doing the complete job or any part thereof. Most of these companies will even furnish the paper. Have your return address printed on both the letterhead and the envelope. If you can afford it, have the whole process of mailing done for you. It is much more important for you to spend your time being interviewed, making appointments, reading and answering newspaper want ads, and enlarging your mailing list. If you want to do just part of the work, insert the name and address in the previously prepared letter, sign it, check for correctness of names and addresses, then seal and stamp the letters.

Use a good bond paper, always white—never a color. Be conservative in the physical makeup of the letters. I recommend the use of the monarch-size stationery because it creates a more personal tone. Sign each letter yourself and have your name typed under your signature. Be *sure* to have your telephone number below the body of the letter on the left side. You will receive many telephone requests to come in for an interview.

Letters That Create Interviews

You should expect nothing of the letters except that they get interviews—good interviews. If your letter has been properly written, it should make your interviews a thousand per cent easier, for the letter will have laid a firm foundation for them.

A broadcast letter should produce about six interviews for each hundred sent out. Often the percentage will go much higher. If the first hundred letters bring in only 4 per cent, that does not mean that the letter was bad. Your next 100 may bring in 8 or 10 per cent. One hundred letters are not a large enough sample.

Sometimes people tell me they have had wonderful response—they have received 30, 50, and even 80 per cent replies. "Replies" count for absolutely nothing. Count only the interview requests. You can regard as an interview a reply that states, "We have your interesting letter, and although we have nothing specific in mind, we would suggest that you drop in when you are in this vicinity. We would like to meet you." The writer is hiding behind a mask. He doesn't want to raise your hopes, but many replies like this lead to real job offers.

You will get a number of replies that enclose application blanks for you to fill out and return. This usually means that your letter has gone down to a clerk in the personnel department. I am often asked what you should do with these applications. Long years of experience have taught me that it is pretty much a waste of time to fill them out, and when you finish you may as well mail them directly to the dead-letter office. Yes, there are a few personnel departments who make a fetish of keeping all applications, building up files that contain thousands of names, and sometimes, months or years after a person has sent in an application, he will be asked if he is still interested in a position with that company. I always wonder what they think the person has been doing in the meantime—gone on relief or been collecting unemployment insurance?

If your letters bring in a low percentage of interview requests, probably it is because the letter should be reviewed and strengthened; often it doesn't take much to strengthen it. Too often the applicant tells how an action was accomplished. Forget the "how." Concentrate instead on giving a measurement of *what* was done. I also find that people want to give their whole life history. This acts like pouring water into good coffee—it dilutes, instead of strengthens, the emphasis on their specialty. Everything must be grooved in a single direction—that is, to make you a specialist—to make you different. For instance, if you are a controller for a manufacturer, place all the emphasis on manufacturing. Mold and keep your letter in that groove. No matter how important you feel your other experiences are, do not bring them up in the letter.

This is borne out by the experience of a man who mailed the following letter:

Mr. John Jones, President
Address

DEAR MR. JONES:
I have just completed my second (and final) tour of duty as an Air Force Production and Procurement Officer.

If your Company is in need of someone for its controller's division, then my educational background, business, and military experience may be of interest to you.

Before being recalled to active duty, I installed a standard cost system for a medium-sized manufacturing company. It resulted in a 20 per cent increase in operating profit during a three-year period of rising costs.

I reduced inventory 25 per cent within a year after installing a material control system and improving production controls. I assisted in the preparation of capital and expense budgets.

I reduced direct labor payroll $10,000 per week. I priced new products by estimating material, labor, and overhead costs. I negotiated loans with banks and insurance companies.

I investigated new products for possible financial investment.

I analyzed potential markets and methods of distribution, estimated costs of manufacturing, and projected capital requirements.

I assisted in the mechanization of billing and accounts receivable.

During World War II, I set up controls over thousands of items of Air Force inventory on I.B.M. equipment.

I was one of several thousand officers specially trained in contract termination and redetermination. I am currently posted on these procedures.

I assisted in the preparation of an Air Force audit manual used to determine manufacturers' compliance with government inventory regulations. I trained and supervised 20 civilian analysts in making audits in contractors' plants.

I graduated from —— School in 1940 where I had courses in accounting, budgetary controls, business statistics, and production controls.

In 1938, I graduated from Johns Hopkins University where I majored in natural sciences including chemistry, physics, and mathematics.

From 1946 to 1949 I attended Stevens Institute of Technology for evening courses in engineering, including practical machine shop operation. Recently, at Pace College, I concentrated in evening courses in corporation taxation and business law.

This is what he wrote to tell me about the results of this letter campaign:

Dear Carl,

As you know, I was rather skeptical of the direct mail approach for finding a job.

After a few Thursday evenings with you, I thought that I had my accomplishments in sufficient shape in résumé form to prepare a letter on my own. I sent the letter out in October to 120 companies and received only one interview. You have a copy of the original letter.

Needless to say, I was discouraged. However, I decided to change the letter along the lines you recommended and sent out 160 more letters. 120 of these went to exactly the same group to whom I originally wrote last October. I also sent out letters to 40 new firms because I wasn't sure that repeating the mailing would accomplish what you said it would.

The response has been terrific. I sent out the letters last Monday and had four interview requests by Tuesday. To date, I have had eight interviews. This letter should pull better than 6 per cent. Better yet, on Thursday I was offered and have since taken a position at $1,800 more than I was making before I was called back into service two years ago. I got the job on the first interview, *without a résumé*, without the company's asking for references, and I received *$2,000 more* than the company originally planned to pay. Strangest of all to me, but I am sure not to you, is that the company *never even bothered to answer the first letter I sent them in October*. Of the interviews to date from this last mailing, all of them have been from companies on the original October list. Some never answered the first letter; others had sent courtesy replies. So it really doesn't make any difference what happened a few months ago.

You have converted me to direct mail. When I was thinking of the possible consequences of making the quick decision I had to make in taking this job, I figured it really didn't make too much difference. I can always send out another 150 letters if things don't work out. It does give you quite a feeling of security.

This second broadcast letter to Mr. John Jones was essentially the same as the one he had sent a month previously, *except* that he deleted this paragraph:

Later, for an investment company, I placed with banks and insurance companies business and mortgage loans ranging from

$10,000 to several million dollars. I analyzed the operating performance of several manufacturers in which the company had financial interests.

You will note that this paragraph placed him with an investment company—a far cry from a manufacturing firm. It took only that short paragraph to dilute his manufacturing experience. He says that for the second mailing he used 160 names. One hundred and twenty of these were from the list he had first used and which had pulled only 1 per cent interviews. He added forty new names to his list because he doubted that the old list would get interviews. However, he did much better with the old list than the new. Note that he says in his letter to me, "The response has been terrific. . . . Of the interviews to date from this last mailing, all of them have been from . . . the original October list." Strangest of all, the company (his new employer) never had bothered to answer the previous letter. You may well ask, "How is this possible?" The answer is that business is ever changing and never static. I will have more to say about this later.

Your Letter Must Make the Reader Drool

When the recipient of your letter reads it, he must drool. He must see something that is close to his interest. Perhaps he has a problem at that moment that must be solved. All businesses, no matter how smoothly they seem to be running to an outsider, are meeting just one problem after another. Some problems are more acute than others, but there will always be problems in sales, taxes, government contracts, costs, new products, public relations, manpower, acquisitions or mergers. It is into this atmosphere that your letter arrives. Your letter states factual deeds which you have accomplished or, in other words, problems which you have solved for someone else. If one of your achievements fits the reader's problem of the moment, your chance of being called in is very good. The interviewer usually brings up the one thing in the letter which struck his interest, so you can readily tell which accomplishment is of most interest to him.

No business stands still; it moves either backward or forward. A small percentage of your letter readers are faced with a particular problem today. Perhaps none of your achievements offers a solution to his problem of the moment, so you do not get a request for an interview. This situation may change completely in a few weeks. Four weeks later, you should send out another letter to those on your list who did not ask you to come in for an interview when they received your first letter. I have found that with almost the same letter you will get about the same percentage of interviews as you got from the first round, sometimes even more.

The Magic Formula

In the 1940's I came across Richard C. Borden's book, *Public Speaking as Listeners Like It* (Harper & Bros.). In it he demonstrates his formula for speech organization and clarity. I then started to apply this formula to letter writing—perhaps crudely—but I consider the results pure magic. Borden says in his book, "Listeners like vertebrate speeches—speeches with a spine. They dislike jellyfish speeches. They dislike flabby, shapeless speeches that begin nowhere, ramble in all directions, and end nowhere." I simply transpose "listeners" to "readers" and "speeches" to "letters." Paraphrased, it becomes "Readers like vertebrate letters—letters with a spine," etc.

Today, every broadcast letter that comes to me for consideration is constructed on these four steps. They are as follows:

Step One   —"Ho Hum"
Step Two   —"Why bring that up?"
Step Three—"For instance"
Step Four —"So what?"

The first, the "Ho Hum" paragraph, must catch the reader's interest immediately. It must make him sit up in his swivel chair; he must react as if you had rung his doorbell.

The second, "Why bring that up?", must build the connective link between your opening paragraph and its application to him or to his business. Here, too, it becomes necessary to show that you are looking for a job and a very specific one. It is quite important that you guide the reader in the direction you want him to go.

In the third step, the "For instance" one, you must give concrete evidence of what you have done. Do not make it a recital of generalizations, but recall your specific *deeds*. I stressed in the earlier chapter on résumés that your résumé be a recital of deeds or, in other words, your measurable "for instances." These now become the main body of your letter.

With your reader up to step four, "So what?", his reaction now will be "What do you want me to do about it?" Now is the time to ask for, or suggest, some action or response which is within his power to give.

Step I. Ho Hum—Opening Paragraphs

A. Topical Openings. I have found only two kinds of opening paragraphs which are effective—topical and accomplishment types of openings. The topical type is much more difficult to find and use than the accomplishment one. I have seen very few really good topical opening paragraphs. Timing and circumstances have a lot to do with this. Still, I recommend the topical if at all possible because of its electrifying effect. Following are some examples of topical openers which pulled interviews far above the normal percentages:

A week ago, I was filling sandbags in London, England. I was still advertising manager of ——— company. All merchandising and advertising had stopped on account of the war.

The writer of this letter had came back to the States to bring his family out of the war zone. He had walked the streets and rung doorbells for two months without getting a job. Then, with my help, he wrote this broadcast letter, using the above opening paragraph. Two weeks later, he was back on a payroll at a higher salary than he had ever earned before.

Another example: "I have come back home to stay after eight years in South America." The timing of this opening was right—business was then looking to South America. It brought the amazing response of 23 per cent of interview requests, in spite of the fact that the writer let it be known that she was not going back to South America and had really come home to stay.

Here is another topical approach: "I sold Florida orange juice to the people of California." I like this one. It was startling—almost like selling a refrigerator to an Eskimo. It was written by an advertising account executive.

Another one:

I have been in Sing Sing prison twenty times—each time in a professional capacity, auditing the books of the prison.

This was used by a seventy-five-year-old certified public accountant whose complete letter appears in a later chapter, "Life Can Begin for You at Fifty—"
Still another:

When peace comes, industry may again, as in 1919, face the necessity of finding supplementary lines to utilize its vast new plant capacity.

This opening seemed very good at the time but brought in a very low percentage of interview requests, because the timing was poor. The person was too early—business wasn't yet giving any thought to postwar planning. But two years later, essentially the same opener brought an above-normal percentage of interviews.

B. *Accomplishment Openings.* Accomplishment type of opening paragraphs I have found to be more useful because they are much more adaptable to different people, whereas the topical depends too much on the right timing and on particular circumstances. Furthermore, in this type of opening, an accomplishment may be lifted out of your résumé. Try to use one that fits the business situation or cycle of the moment. For instance, in the last few years, the business world had problems about reducing its inventory position, so the following example was sent out at just the right time:

As an assistant controller, I set up controls which decreased inventory one million dollars in just 12 months. This was done even though sales had increased during this period by $5,000,000.

Though the writer of this letter had been only an assistant controller up to this time, he landed a full controllership.
Here is an opener for a completely different sort of job:

As a National Convention Manager, I helped develop an electronic product display which drew more than 50,000 visitors to our booth.

The man who wrote this is now with a computer company as assistant to the president.

Other examples:

Marketing Manager
a) As an Assistant Marketing Manager for a leading consumer product, I helped increase sales 12 per cent through a new marketing policy.

Financial Manager
b) I recently brought a 25 million dollar contract under financial control within a period of two months—and, more important, at a substantial increase in net profit.

This person is now the financial vice-president of his company.

Two accomplishment openers used by controllers read:

As Controller and Treasurer of a medium-sized manufacturing company, I converted a previous operating loss situation into a net profit of 15 per cent of sales, before taxes.

As Assistant Controller of a manufacturing company doing 25 million in sales, I discovered neglected stock, sold it for $240,000 and thus made a profit of $30,000 instead of taking a loss of $60,000.

The man who wrote this letter is now controller of a well-known company.

A salesperson opened with, "As territorial salesman for an industrial goods manufacturer, I increased sales in my territory 20 per cent in just one year."

A retailer opened his letter by saying, "As a merchandise manager in a large Midwestern department store, I doubled the volume of business in the basement 'ready-to-wear' section in four years. My profits were 10 per cent above the store's average."

You see how easy it is to get a striking opening paragraph. In your résumé you will find many which are just as potent. In the examples I have given, you will notice that nearly every person mentions his specialty. Also mark how the opening sentence gives the direction in which the writer wants to go, by mentioning his title and telling what function he performed.

Step II. Why Bring That Up?

Once you have succeeded in arousing the reader's interest, you must now answer his unasked questions: "Why are you bringing this up? What has it to do with me or my company? Why are you writing to me?" Your second paragraph must tell *why*. You can answer these questions by being completely frank in telling exactly why you are writing to him. For instance:

I am writing to you because your company may be in need of a man for its blank department with my training and experience. If so, you may be interested in other things I have done.

Following are examples of different ways to phrase the second paragraph, depending on what the job interest is. In all cases the "I am writing you because" is implied.

1. Your company may need someone in the controller's or financial department. My experience may interest you.

2. If your company needs a Manufacturing Manager with my training and experience, you may be interested in some of the things I have accomplished.

3. Your company may have need in your marketing operation for someone with my experience.

4. If you need sales representation, you may be interested in some of the other things I have done.

5. Your company may be in need of a sales executive. If so, you may be interested in what I have done in sales.

6. Your company may be planning to develop its foreign trade and may, therefore, be interested in my experience and background.

7. If your company is in need of someone with budget and control experience, you may be interested in what I have done as a Budget and Control Manager.

Step III. For Instance—Show Me Why I Should Be Interested

This is the time to use the "for instances" you developed in your résumé. You can now lift three, four, or even five right out of the context, if you developed the résumé as suggested. The following letter was written to a medium-sized manufacturing company. It brought interviews from all over the country. Some of the prospective employers were so anxious to interview this man they offered to pay his travel expenses. We lifted his deeds for his third step right out of his résumé:

If your company needs a man of my experience for your manufacturing or engineering operations, you may be interested in what I have done. I have:

Doubled the plant area and relocated it without loss of production. Under my direction, $200,000 of priority equipment was procured for a new plant layout.

In a tight labor market, I expanded the production staff 150 per cent and doubled the professional staff.

While Chief Engineer, I expanded the market by improving the product. This secured new sales of high temperature and high load applications not previously possible.

I doubled the commercial applications in two years and directed low-cost design, which established the product in the field of machine tools and motor boats.

I provided a field engineering service, models, test installations, and catalogue data. New sales of highly engineered applications were secured through these services.

Precautions: Use only one deed or one "for instance" to a paragraph. Let each example stand out as if you had thrown a sponge of wet paint against a canvas. Do not try to condense two or more ideas into a single paragraph. No artist would ever put two pictures in the same frame.

Remember my advice on résumé writing. It applies here, too, and is even more important. Try to use no more than ten to twelve words in a sentence. Keep all paragraphs down to three and not more than four lines. Work and rework them until you achieve the greatest strength—a smooth staccato.

Step IV. So What?

Before you proceed with this step, put in a paragraph mentioning your educational background—schools, graduate schools, or colleges. Do not mention any kind of training—it may affect the intended direction of your letter. Mentioning your schools however adds to the reader's receptivity; it ties you to a known-quality label.

Then proceed to the last step, Step IV, the close of your letter, in which you must ask or suggest action which is within the power of the reader to give. Since the whole purpose of the letter is to secure an interview, you now suggest that interview somewhat in the following manner:

I should be glad to discuss further details of my business experience in a personal interview,

or:

If you desire to discuss my experience in greater detail, I shall be glad to do so in a personal interview.

A note of warning: Do *not* end your letter with:

I enclose a résumé of my business experience. I would appreciate an opportunity to discuss any possible position which you may have in your organization.

for the following reasons:

1. If you mention the résumé at all, he will probably ask you to mail it, and you will have lost the interview.
2. "I would appreciate" suggests begging. You should not beg for an interview. It is not necessary.
3. Never say "discuss any possible position that you may have to offer." This weakens your whole letter. Remember you are selling yourself in one position, your specialty. To ask for any position makes you a surplus commodity and decreases your demand product value.
4. Never say, "I would like to show you how I can help increase your profits." He will, and rightly, consider this presumptuous, coming from an outsider.
5. Never address the letter to anyone except the president. You can always find his name in the directories. Only he knows whether or not he plans to retire a treasurer, controller, etc.

Tips on Sources for Mailing Lists

Develop your own mailing list; do not buy one from professional list-sellers. Some name lists may have as many as five or six names in the same company. To have your letter go out to all these could only spell disaster. Usually, when you pay for a list, it is not turned over to you, but is used by the list-seller to mail your letter for you. This means you never find out how many firms on the list "can't be found" or have "moved, left no address." As many as 10 to 15 per cent of your letters may be wasted.

Make your list strong by selecting your own names. No one but *you* knows the size and kind of company you want to work for. No one but *you* knows the geographical location you prefer. Only *you* can determine whether a large or small company can afford your job activity. For instance, a small company cannot afford electronic data processing.

List of Books to Use in Making Up Your Mailing List

Poor's Register of Corporations, Directors, and Executives. This has a geographical listing. It is the best for all-round use.

News Front Magazine. Register of 12,000 companies. It can be purchased for $6.00.

Dun & Bradstreet's "Million Dollar Directory." This has a monthly supplement to keep it up to date. It is very productive.

Standard Register. This is published by the National Association of advertisers. It is extremely useful for people in marketing.

Moody's Banks, Insurance, Real Estate and Investment Trusts is good for people who are exploring these fields.

State Directories. Every state's Department of Commerce publishes a directory. These are available by writing to this department in specific states.

Regional and City Directories. There is one put out by the New England Council. The Boston Chamber of Commerce puts out a *Directory of Manufacturers*. Check with your own Chamber of Commerce. They may have what you need. These local directories are effective when you want to concentrate on a particular area.

Proof of the Effectiveness of the Broadcast Letter

Here is one of thousands of letters received by the author from those he has helped:

DEAR CARL:

After having tried for years to persuade you to write a book on your experiences in helping executives find the kind of jobs they are looking for, I should have been among the first to send you a letter expressing my views on the subject. I certainly want to apologize for my misconduct in not writing sooner and hope that this letter has not reached you too late and that it may serve a useful purpose. Actually, I have resolved no less than 100 times to write this letter but have had a peculiar mental block, worse than preparing an income tax return, because it concerns myself and trying to tell the next fellow how to do better than the little I have done. Accordingly, I seek your forgiveness.

You have mentioned that some people feel that putting on a direct mail campaign when they are seeking a job is beneath their dignity and that it puts them in a menial position. I must confess that I felt exactly the same way until I learned otherwise.

After I recovered from the astonishment of finding that the world was not avidly seeking somebody with my specific experience or qualifications or age or salary level or whatnot, I decided to follow your advice. Besides, what I had considered to be an impregnable financial position was beginning to appear less so as each month went by.

Accordingly, I sat down and prepared a letter along the lines recommended by you. After a great deal of work, and many rewrites, the letter was reduced from ten pages to less than two pages and it concentrated on accomplishments instead of the textbook type of experience and personal appraisals.

I sent the letter to about 200 presidents or chairmen of a varied group of companies of a size and character where I thought I might be a likely candidate. About 130 replies were received, but most of these were "regrets" that there was no opening. About 7 asked for an Outline of Experience which I then sent to them and from whom I never heard further. (I have since learned that this is strictly par for the course.) Five gave me interviews. I needed only one job and this I obtained in less than two months of negotiations.

With respect to the company that hired me, they first of all had me talk with two of their vice-presidents, then they sent the company plane to have me visit headquarters, and subsequently I talked with a director who was a partner of a large investment banking firm and also with a partner of the company's accounting firm.

The job I obtained was that of General Sales Manager of a company doing $200,000,000 sales with 3,400 people in the sales department.

The company had been looking almost two years for a man with certain specifications to fill this job. It so happened that I had the kind of specifications they thought they had in mind, and my letter fortunately reached them at the right time.

The appointment was published in approximately 300 publications, including *The New York Times,* Chicago *Tribune*, Los Angeles *Times*, etc., and in most instances a photograph accompanied the notice.

Compensation was in the six-figure range.

In looking back on the situation it seems to me that the reception given me by the five companies who granted interviews was excellent in all respects. I simply explained what I liked about each of their companies and accordingly why I had written. Without exception, there was a favorable response to my reason and also to the direct action approach. By comparison, I did not have the feeling of having my hat in my hand and being given the condescending treatment that I had previously experienced, all too often, when friends passed me on to friends.

About the only exception I can think of is that a recommendation is a highly effective way of making a change when a person has no need for changing a job. If the need arises, then the converse suddenly becomes true.

Inasmuch as very few people who need a job can afford a false sense of dignity in lieu of a job, I strongly recommend a well-worded letter in a direct mail campaign. The sooner this approach is taken the better, so that the lapse of time between jobs does not weaken one's position.

I will repeat what I once told you; namely, that if you want to refer anyone to me, I will be glad to straighten them out on the subject of the type of treatment one receives on interviews resulting from a direct mail campaign.

In conclusion, I can only say that I have talked with others who have tried out the direct letter approach and we've all had the same type of experience, as indicated above.

Now that I have got this letter written, I will once again not be afraid to walk into the ——— Club where I might bump into you. I hope you will recognize me.

With my best regards,

Sincerely,
David

Sample Broadcast Letter

Here is an example of a complete broadcast letter showing steps I, II, III, and IV. Notice the short paragraphs and the short staccato sentences. This letter brought results. Yours can too.

As Sales Manager for a manufacturing firm, I increased sales by 23%. Every dollar of this increase was profitable.

You may be interested in a man with my marketing and sales management experience. Here are some of the other things I have done:

Launched a new product. Triggered first year sales of $3 million in new markets.

Introduced a style element into a commodity product. Accelerated company leadership, consumer acceptance and trade-mark identity. Stretched profit by 8%.

Recruited and trained salesmen. These men are among the top producers of the company.

Developed an average customer into the top account in the nation—exceeding combined sales of the four top customers.

Forecasted sales with 90% accuracy. Achieved greater return on capital investment in plant and inventory.

Crystallized the corporate marketing strategy which moved sales from $26 million to $54 million in five years.

I am a graduate of the ———— Business School where I specialized in sales management and marketing.

I will be happy to discuss further details of my experience with you in a personal interview.

Very truly yours,

CHAPTER 4

How to Get Interviews Through Advertisers

REMEMBER that in your job campaign I rate broadcast letters first in importance. I rate second, answering ads found in the "Positions Open" and "Help Wanted" columns appearing in the classified and business sections of the daily papers. These are a very productive source for creating interviews. Every daily newspaper carries some of these ads. *The New York Times* is exceptionally good on the East Coast. *The Wall Street Journal*, now published in major cities across the country, is another excellent source. Every locality will have one or more newspapers which are better than others. These will be the papers you will use to look for jobs in a certain locality. Do not overlook trade magazines. Do not overlook *any* publication that carries classified "Job Openings." If you need help, your local librarian will be happy to assist you. It doesn't matter where or how you find the ads. The important thing is that you find them and answer them. If the ads' descriptions come anywhere near your job sphere or specialty, you have nothing to lose but your time and postage. *Remember*, you are in a campaign, so explore all the avenues.

Blind Ads

Most ads are blind. Not more than 2 per cent of the advertisers do so under their own names. You will be requested to write to a box number of the particular newspaper. Ninety-nine per cent of the ads will request that you mail a résumé. Here are a couple of examples:

Send complete résumé of background to ———, N.Y. Times ———.

Send a complete résumé detailing your personal education, employment history, and salary requirements. Box ———, Wall Street Journal.

Omit Your Résumé and Get a 25 Per Cent Return

Never send your résumé to an advertiser. Do not do so even though he requests you to. Do not do so even though almost every article and every book on job-finding advises you to do just this. Sending a résumé is suicidal for getting an interview. It would be better for you to lose a possible interview than to mail your résumé. You will make this up later through the greater number of interviews.

Over the years I have known people who have answered thousands of these ads. They mailed covering letters and enclosed résumés as requested. I can assure you from my years of experience that the percentage of those called in for interviews is very small. It is well below 1 per cent. This means 100 letters to get just one interview.

I have been told by the personnel director of a large organization which advertises constantly that every ad brings in hundreds and sometimes thousands of replies. These get culled down to a relatively small number to be called in for interviews. If your answer to the ad doesn't single you out so that you stand apart as that one in a hundred or a thousand, you have little chance of being called in.

Therefore, when you answer an ad, simply send a letter similar to, or an adaptation of, your broadcast letter. The returns from such a letter show a phenomenal increase over the answers which include résumés. You will now get one interview for every four letters, or 25 per cent reaction. Sometimes you will get four replies from ten letters. In a recent job campaign, over a four-month period, out of a hundred ads answered this way, twenty-one resulted in interviews. Answering advertisements is actually more productive on a percentage basis than sending out broadcast letters.

Do Not Depend on Ads Alone

You may ask, therefore, why you should not answer ads exclusively. I would recommend this were it not for the fact that there are altogether too few ads. You do not get sufficient interview exposure, and the waiting time is too long between ads. You cannot afford the time, money, or the deterioration of your morale to wait for advertisers; hence, you must obtain most of your interviews by what I call the *active and aggressive approach—broadcast letters*. This is the reason I rate them of first importance in your job campaign.

Then, too, during periods of depression or recession, there

is a decided falling off in the number of "Job Open" advertisements. Can you afford to wait out a depression? Broadcast letters, for some unaccountable reason, bring in as many interview invitations in bad as in good times. This is another reason why broadcast letters are of first importance.

There is also another important reason. Many worthwhile positions are for months in the embryonic or incubating stage in the mind of the boss. These are openings in the making. They are in the talking or "we must do something about this" stage. Perhaps his banker, public accounting firm, or management consultant has pointed out such a necessity, and may have even made prodding suggestions. Sometimes an executive is approaching compulsory retirement in a few years. A successor must be trained. These situations are often weeks and even months away from the action stage before someone finally decides to advertise, get in touch with employment agencies, or pass the word around to sources likely to produce the right person.

Time and again the broadcast letters have fallen on this kind of virgin territory and people have been called in for interviews. No one except the president and one or two others, sometimes not even the personnel department, knew that the management was considering adding to the staff or replacing someone with a stronger person. Often the actual job requirements have not been made definitive.

It is within this area that your broadcast letters count, so don't sit around and wait for advertisements to appear. It is action and continuous action that counts. It creates the momentum that brings in the job you really want.

When you see a job advertisement, you know there is an opening. Surely, no one would spend up to several hundred dollars advertising just for the fun of it. You also get a pretty fair inkling of the kind of job that is waiting. Sometimes the ad will outline definite functional experience wanted. This, then, is your opportunity. You now have a chance through your answering letter to show that *you* are the person they are seeking. Make your letter so outstanding that you will be that *one in a hundred* called in for the interview.

This is the time when most job-seekers will run for their pens and papers immediately and write a letter explaining what they think they can do for this employer. They attach their résumés, which undoubtedly are of the functional and subjective self-appraisement type.

Avoid a Self-Appraisement Answer

The following letter was sent to the officer of a company which advertised under its own name instead of using a blind box number. *Avoid making this kind of response:*

Dear Sirs:

I have read your advertisement and enclose a résumé as requested. Yours is an organization where I believe my full potential for business accomplishment could be achieved with outstanding performance satisfaction to you and to me. Types of work responsibilities in your field should make an unusual blending with my greatest interests and abilities.

After fifteen years of varied business experience, I have come to the realization that a combination of research and analytical writing with the objective of contributing to the wide distribution of worthwhile business and general information is the activity in which I can find my greatest satisfaction.

My graduation from ———— University gives you assurance that I am good material for eventual participation in administrative policy-making activities.

May I have the opportunity to see you or some one of your organization at a place and time convenient to you to discuss the possibility of my entering your company? An affirmative reply will be very much appreciated.

                                        Very truly yours,

The company official who received this letter mailed it to me with the following comments:

This letter seems to me to violate all principles of tact and diplomacy. Does this man really think that he can step in and run our business on a very short notice? Does this man think our business exists solely as a place where he can "realize his full potential for business accomplishment"? Does this man think that his interest and progress constitute the hub around which the universe revolves?

I hope none of you will write a letter anything like this— not after what I have stressed in the previous chapters. I want to add two comments to the ones outlined above.

1. When the answering letter says, ". . . types of work . . . should make an unusual blending with my greatest interests and abilities," my reaction is "Nuts, who cares about the blending of *his* greatest interests and abilities?"

2. Neither a college degree, a master's degree, nor a Ph.D. gives an employer the assurance that you are of management or executive caliber. It takes more than scholastic excellence to do that. If you are just out of school, an employer may give you a chance to prove yourself. After that, you will be measured by your *performance*.

The close of the letter is what I call the "tin cup" or "panhandling" approach. Never use such words as "May I have the opportunity . . ." It sounds too much like "Brother, can you spare a dime?" Also, never say, "An affirmative reply will be greatly appreciated."

Take Aim

When you see a "position open" advertisement which comes within the scope of your experience, someone has been good enough to set up a target for you to shoot at. A very small percentage of ads may fit your qualifications perfectly. There will perhaps be some little requirement which you feel excludes you. This could be age, education, salary, or experience in a different industry. Do not presume, therefore, that it is of no use for you to answer that ad. Don't take it for granted that you will be ruled out. Let the prospective employer make that decision. If he doesn't want you, he will say "No" or refuse to answer.

I wish I were able to recount the number of people who wind up with a job in a company after answering an ad which they thought was not quite in their line or was out of their reach. They had decided in advance for some flimsy reason that the ad excluded them. Job descriptions generally are so broad that it is impossible for any individual to meet *all* the specifications. There nearly always has to be a compromise. Don't forget that even the person who is finally chosen for the job will not have all the qualifications; so answer those ads and give yourself an extra chance at an interview.

Answering ads is like competing in a turkey shoot. There is a long line in back of you and each person is waiting for a turn to shoot at the target. Advertisements in *The Wall Street Journal*, *The New York Times*, and other papers are read over the entire United States. Is it any wonder then that advertisers may receive 500 or even 1,000 answers? In this kind of competition, it would seem that you have an almost impossible task, when you write a letter that will result in your being selected as one of the persons to be interviewed.

When you answer an ad, you are always subjected to this kind of competition. This is much heavier competition than you get from a broadcast letter, where you may be the only one who has written about a certain job.

Be Specific

With an advertisement in front of you, "you are now on target." Remember, you get only one shot and no more. Therefore, your answer had better be good. Your letter must be specific. It should leave a sharp, concrete image. It should make the same clear, singular impression that a rifle shot leaves in a target. Do not let your letter be like a blast from a shotgun, which would leave a blurred image. In this situation, it is difficult, I know, to refrain from including in the letter your entire experience and background. Perhaps you hope that one small pellet from the blast might make a hit.

Time and again someone will say to me, "I thought I might be called in for something else when he read about my broad over-all experience." This is not impossible but highly improbable. In reality things don't work out that way. The advertisement that asks for a specialist demands specific experience. If the advertiser wanted a jack-of-all-trades, he would say so.

Writing the Letter

You are now ready to write the letter. It should conform to the "miracle" formula explained in the chapter on letter writing. The context should be so interesting and compelling that, after the opening paragraph, the reader will want to finish the letter and decide then and there that he cannot afford not to see you. Many advertisements are worded in a very general way. In instances like these, it is possible to use your regular broadcast letter when you answer, without altering it in any way. Simply address the letter to the box number or to the address in the ad. And, I repeat, do not include your résumé.

Next, there are the ads which outline certain functional experience requirements. It is most important that you spell out each function mentioned in the ad. Now, take out your résumé, an all-important factor in helping you to answer ads. I called your résumé your personal Sears catalog out of which you can draw the necessary deeds or "for instances." It is not necessary that you list your accomplishments in the same chronological order that they were performed. Instead, follow the functional requirements outlined in the ad, with one concrete "for instance" after another. Include some measurements or figures for each, if you can possibly do so.

Your opening sentence should be of the same "make 'em sit up and take notice" variety I suggested for your broadcast letter. In fact, wherever possible use the one you finally worked out so carefully for the broadcast letter.

Following is an ad and an answering letter. You will note that the ad lists seven functional requirements—more than one usually finds in an ad:

MARKETING RESEARCH

ARE YOU SEEKING
REAL CHALLENGE
—for—

creating ways of expanding current marketing efforts
evaluating distribution methods and channels
analyzing competitive marketing policies and practices
determining market potentials for new products
studying territorial potentials and profitability

conducting actual field experiments with new marketing techniques
recommending broad marketing policy thru personal contact with top management?
We are a diversification-minded Philadelphia company with sales of a half-billion dollars thru both retail and industrial channels. If you have a creative marketing mind, experience in the above areas, and probably an MBA degree, we would like to talk to you about becoming MANAGER OF THE SPECIAL PROJECTS DIVISION of our Market Research and Planning Department. Send your complete résumé and an indication of salary requirements in confidence to H-84, P.O. Box 2066, Phila. 3, Pa. Our present staff knows of this ad. We are an equal opportunity employer.

This is an excellent example of an applicant's letter in reply to such an ad:

GENTLEMEN:
I have initiated and managed all your seven Marketing Research Projects as an operating executive and as a consultant, producing the following results:
Turned a long-term loss in the first profit for a 30-year-old line of 100 sea foods;
Established a profitable market in industry and 7 new channels for a 75-year-old household chemical firm;
Laid out a five-year program to increase sales by $19 millions for an aluminum producer;
Programmed sales expansions from under $2 million to over $8 million, realized by two national brand manufacturers;
I specialized in Marketing and Research at ——— Graduate School of Business after graduation from ——— College. My compensation ideas check out as competitive.
I will be glad to go over the direct applications of my experience to your opportunities in a meeting with you personally.

I call your particular attention to the opening paragraph and the four examples which follow. The opening paragraph sounds like a man with great qualifications and ability who is then willing to follow up his positive approach with *specific* "for instances." Note that he neither mentions nor includes a résumé. He did not state a salary requirement. The result of this letter was that he was called to New York for an appointment. Apparently the "for instances" were too compelling to be tossed into the wastebasket. Try to write a similar letter, so that you will be the "one in a thousand" who will be called in for an interview.

The following ad was answered by another man. He was told during the course of his interview that the employer had received 1,500 replies. The very first screening resulted in 1,400 of the 1,500 being tossed into the wastebasket. This left only 100, or about 6 per cent, of men who had answered the ad to be interviewed. Out of these 100 only 10 were called in for final, intensive interviews and tests, and out of these 10 three were left to compete for the job opening. Here is the ad and the answer that resulted in this man's being selected for an interview.

AN ADVENTURE IN MANAGEMENT

We are looking for Executive Talent to provide the management nucleus for a new multi-million dollar organization. The positions are of prime responsibility at Vice-Presidential level with outstanding opportunity for continual growth.

Our Mid-West client is the largest manufacturer of its products in an expanding industry. It is organizing a wholly-owned subsidiary to manufacture and market a related product line based on major advances in design and production methods.

We need several executives with minimum prior earnings of

$20,000.00 per year. These men must be able to function with a group that will welcome the challenge of devising new and unconventional management methods. We want broad rather than specialized experience, with emphasis on Manufacturing, Marketing, or Finance.

Send complete résumé with salary requirements

This is the reply:

DEAR SIR:

Since you are seeking executives with broad management experience in manufacturing, marketing, and finance, you may be interested in some of my qualifications.

As President and General Manager of a medium-sized manufacturing company, I doubled the output and net worth within three years.

Developed a new sales organization and marketing program which brought in two years' backlog of new business. Won for the company its largest engineering contract in 7 years against industry-wide competition.

Secured $2 million new equity capital from numerous private sources.

Completed a $4 million engineering development of the company's principal product.

As Director of Finance of a large multi-plant manufacturing company, I developed profit plans and conducted financial negotiations for $200 million of sub-contracts. In one year, I turned a 7-year-loss-history into a profit.

Originated an increment cost analysis. Then carried out negotiations which prevented the termination of $50 million of contracts. Saved $3 million in net income.

As Senior Associate of a leading New York firm of consulting engineers, I planned a manufacturing program involving 10,000 employees. Prevented the loss of millions of dollars worth of contracts which had been hopelessly behind schedule.

Increased consolidated net profit 25 per cent of a large industrial company through cost reductions and improved efficiency.

I am a graduate of the ———— School where I majored in Financial Management. Am also technically trained with an engineering degree and several years of engineering practice.

I would be glad to discuss my experience further in a personal interview.

Sincerely yours,

Let us review this letter briefly. Note that he mentions *specifically* each function asked for in the ad: 1) Broad management in manufacturing, marketing, and finance; 2) Engineering design; 3) Production methods; 4) Devised new management methods. He mentions each of these with a quantitative "for instance."

Note also that the advertisement specified "send a complete résumé" and "salary requirements." Both these items were purposely ignored in the answering letter.

Nevertheless, the letter resulted in this man's being selected out of 1,500 who answered the ad.

I would like to stress again that it is most important that you answer all functional requirements. Do not merely answer them, but restate each function.

You may be up against someone who has been delegated to do the original screening. The screener may have been given an outline to guide him in selecting which answers to keep and which he can afford to throw away. Therefore, if your letter answers all the requirements, you will probably be in for the first round of interviews. Often the screener does this so mechanically that he may not realize he is doing it.

It is good salesmanship (and should be regarded as such) on

your part to restate each one of the functional requirements mentioned in the ad. Every salesman has been taught that it is absolutely necessary to let the prospect know that he understands his questions and objections. Otherwise the prospective buyer may build up a negative reaction and feel that the salesman is trying to gloss over the answers to the questions because he has no specific answers. Therefore, a good salesman answers by first repeating the question in the buyer's own words. So when you answer an ad in the same way, you are just applying common-sense salesmanship.

The man who answered this ad kept a close tab on his replies. He told me that when he answers an ad which has a specific requirement, such as financial vice-president, he gets a 15 per cent interview reply to his letters. When he answers ads that state broad general requirements, necessitating answers that are not so specific, his interview requests drop to 8 per cent. This bears out my previous statement—the more specific you are in your answer, the greater will be the number of interviews you secure. The following letter is another good example of being specific about your specialty:

GENTLEMEN:

I originated rental of light equipment in this area. Prior to this, my market analysis guided an industrial leasing company in a 100% growth.

Are you looking for a man who can produce your share of sales in the rental and leasing markets? If you are, you may be interested in some of my experiences.

A general renting company I pioneered here does a volume equal to that of much older companies of similar size.

With a large leasing company, I discovered a potential $30 million market. The market study I wrote was instrumental in obtaining the long-term money needed.

The trend to leasing was demonstrated in a booklet written by me. Mailings of the booklet quintupled leads and resulted in over $1 million in purchase lease-back business.

I graduated from the ——— Business School in Management in 1950 and from ——— College in Science in 1948.

I would be happy to give you more information in a personal interview.

> Very truly yours,

The above letter was used by this man both as a broadcast letter and as his answer to advertisements without any alterations. Here is what he wrote me:

This letter was mailed to about 200 presidents. Half of these were repeat mailings and drew 6 per cent interviews. This letter, when used to answer ads, was almost 100 per cent effective.

Would you like to know the results of this man's campaign? He took a job with a large international leasing corporation as Eastern sales manager. He expects to be the national sales manager in a few months. I quote again from his letter: "Declined two positions and am still being sought after by two major companies."

I hope these examples have shown you how to answer advertisements. Now get to work on your letter.

1. Use your regular broadcast letter, making use of the box number of the newspaper as the address.
2. Use the broadcast letter except for the second paragraph where you refer to the ad and the position.
3. Take the ad apart. For each functional requirement, mention a concrete deed with some numerical measurement.

4. Never mention salary. It would be better for you to leave that for the interview.

Eventually, your answers can be part of answers you may have used previously. For instance, one job-seeker numbered his letters consecutively and then assigned a number to each paragraph. Then, when a letter was needed, a secretary would use paragraph number____in letter____to answer a specific ad. This saved an immense amount of time.

Recently, I talked over the phone to a management consultant of Stamford, Connecticut. He uses newspaper ads to a great extent to attract applicants for jobs he is trying to fill. He said this: "I receive hundreds of letters and résumés in answer to my newspaper advertisements. I am shocked and it breaks my heart to have to toss most of them in the wastebasket. I am sure there must be many excellent men in my discards, but I haven't the time to find this out. Their letters are too vague to be of any help to me."

Now go to it. Answer every ad that seems to come within your sphere. Your letters will get better and more concise and to the point as you go along.

Jolt the Advertisers With a Reminder

After you have answered advertisements you should receive requests for interviews. Some will come in immediately, others will be delayed depending on the number who answered the advertisement.

If you have not received an answer to a job that seemed perfect for your experience, try the following two or three weeks later. Mail a copy of your letter to the same box number of the same paper with a covering letter somewhat as follows,

DEAR SIR:

I answered your ad of ———— date in the ———— paper. I felt reasonably sure that I had most of the qualifications you wanted. Perhaps my letter did not reach you. I am, therefore, taking the liberty of enclosing a xeroxed copy. I doubt that you can ascertain my qualifications and personality very well from a written page. May I suggest again a personal interview at your convenience?

Sincerely,
Sarah Hunter

The above has been tried by quite a number of people and has proven to be very effective. There may have been so many answers that yours may have been overlooked. Give them another chance.

CHAPTER 5

Placing Job-Wanted Advertisements

MY FIRST EXPERIENCE with advertising goes back some twenty years. Lewis L. had been merchandise manager of a large department store in Chicago. He had been looking for a job for several months. One evening he asked for my opinion about placing an ad in *Women's Wear Daily*. During the next three or four days there was to be a National Retail Dry Goods Association convention and he reasoned that the time had come for his big chance. All the big store executives would be in town. Further, he reasoned, they would all be reading this publication, so his chances of getting some good interviews out of such an ad ought to be good.

He showed me the ad he had prepared. It was well written, of display size—large enough to be noticed. He told me it would cost him over $100. I explained to him that these men were at a convention, had meetings during the day and at night would probably be going to shows and night clubs. In all probability, during their spare time, they would be drinking, eating, and dancing—certainly would not be sitting alone in a hotel room reading *Women's Wear*, clipping his ad, and then rushing to the phone to ask him for an interview. This had never entered his head.

I added that I thought he would be wasting his money, for when people attended conventions they were too busy. Even if people saw his ad it was not likely that they would act upon it at that time; and if they did nothing about it at that time, they probably never would.

The following morning Lewis L. called me to say he had decided to place the ad anyway. I answered that I hoped it would bring results; in any case, it was a noble experiment. I asked him to tabulate the results for the benefit of others.

A day went by, a second, a third, then a whole week. Each day he called at the newspaper office for his expected answers. No answers ever came in—not a single one. Lewis L. was a very disappointed man.

It was then that I finally persuaded him to use his broadcast letter. He had continually argued against the idea, saying that hiring wasn't done that way in the department-store field.

In spite of this, he mailed several hundred letters the following week to department-store presidents over the entire country. This letter literally exploded into interviews, and he was invited to places as far away as Texas, Oklahoma, and Canada.

The interview he had in Ottawa, Canada, proved to be the gold mine. A family-owned department store was in trouble. It had been run by a father and his son. The father was ill and in the hospital, and the son needed help. Lewis L. was interviewed by the son in the morning and by the father (in the hospital) in the afternoon. Before five o'clock the same day, he was offered the job. He was at work a week later.

I have in front of me copies of the New York *Women's Wear Daily* and the *News Record*. Each carried Lewis L.'s picture and announcement that he now was general merchandise manager of this Canadian store. Just another "miracle."

The advertisement mentioned in the beginning of this chapter cost more money than did the letter campaign. The ad pulled nothing, but the letters did the trick. If he had mailed out letters immediately, he would have saved himself a lot of grief. Lewis was like many others for he was a skeptic in the broadcast-letter method, and he had to be converted.

Many more people have since placed ads in the "Job Wanted" columns of the daily papers. Of all the people I have worked with, I do not know of a single one who was satisfied with the results.

One man wrote me a very detailed report on his job-getting experience. He is the only one who had a goodly number of replies from ads. The following ad appeared in the financial section of the Sunday *New York Times*. It cost $23 for one insertion. The result was eighteen answers but no job.

COST ACCOUNTANT PRODUCTION PLANNER

Business School graduate, former Navy Lt. Commander commanding own ship, age 30, previous experience in production, planning, desires factory accounting position with future. Would consider assistant controller, small company.
Y 2205 Times

That year there was a labor shortage in certain industries. Business was looking for men to hire. Personnel people searched through newspapers. Employment agencies were active in this hunt. Many of them wrote to the "Job Wanted" advertisers.

When you are in a seller's market as far as jobs are concerned, you may do much better with the number of replies you get to your ad, but you will also do much better at such times in the number of replies you will get to your letter campaigns.

The following letter is from another man relating his experience with advertising:

DEAR CARL:

Here is further proof about the uselessness of advertisements. I placed this ad in the Sunday edition of a New York paper seven weeks ago. Up to now I have received not one single reply.

Sincerely,

INT'L MANAGEMENT EXEC

Plan organize and direct your operations. Diversified background in finance marketing manufacturing concentration in Europe common market and Latin America. Market development licensing acquisitions diversification negotiations world wide background with education and career specialization in international commercial operations Harvard MBA reply.
F576 Times.

If you feel you must advertise, be dignified and conservative. Give the future employer one or two good concrete examples of accomplishments, with measurable results.

Recently I asked one of my men whether he had done any advertising in getting his job. He had just gotten a position as overseas sales manager for a drug manufacturer. This is what he told me: "In scanning advertisements in the papers for jobs that fitted me, I also used to look over the ads of men advertising for jobs. In this way, I ran across the ads of three men who had experience similar to my own. I wrote to each one of them. I offered to share the job leads which did not interest me any longer in return for similar leads from them. I also asked them to let me know what their experience had been in getting interviews through the ads." He stated further, "I heard from two of them. Each one was thoroughly disgusted with the results obtained. They stated that they had heard from people offering to sell them name lists; others offered résumé construction for a fee; others had letter printing and addressing to sell. The majority offered a job in return for a financial investment in their business."

Here is another letter in answer to my request for information on the value of advertising for a job:

DEAR CARL:

I am writing to you with reference to the information that you wanted about my experience with "position wanted" ads. In accordance with your advice on the conducting of a campaign, I proceeded to do in a routine fashion everything you advised. First, prepare a résumé, then a solicitation letter, obtain a mailing list and send out letters. At that time, instead of waiting for replies announcing fabulous new offers or for my fairy godmother to intervene with a perfect proposition, I proceeded to take any other action that would have a contributory effect on my objective—namely, call on all executive recruiters, register at all interesting employment agencies and, thirdly, if financially able, insert a Position Wanted advertisement.

At the same time, I sent a Form Letter that appeared as a personal letter to other Position Wanted advertisers and stated that as my background and interests were somewhat similar, I was also advertising and at the same time conducting a mailing campaign using the enclosed Form Letter; and that I would be very interested in exchanging experiences or possible leads if they would care to get in touch with me.

As a result of sending out about seventy-five of these letters, I was contacted by long-distance phone and received letters from all over the United States. The men who wrote said that they would contact me when they came to New York and would then exchange ideas about job hunting. The consensus was that the advertisements were a complete waste of money. Almost everyone experienced the same result in getting replies. Most of them were from people who wanted to run our campaigns for us or to write our résumés, usually at exorbitant prices; or from life insurance salesmen asking for an appointment to discuss life insurance. In addition, many of the men received junk mail, advertising many different items for purchase. Occasionally fly-by-night promoters would have a hot scheme to discuss, usually involving an investment of money, or working time.

Sincerely,

In the final analysis this man secured his job through a mail campaign.

Recently someone brought me the following advertisement:

BOSS WANTED
BY YOUNG MAN ON WAY DOWN
WHO WANTS TO GO BACK UP.

9 Years Top Publication Experience—Space Sales, Sales Prom., Merchandising. College Degree, plus 2 Yrs. of Graduate Work. 32, Mar. & Family. Finest Ref.

I don't know how this advertiser made out—whether or not he was given a chance for a comeback. My immediate reaction was, "What is wrong with this man? Did he fall into the cellar and needs someone to pull him out? What was it that pulled him down? Why does he have to go to this length?" There are too many negative reactions created in the reader's mind for such an ad to be useful.

"Situation Wanted" ads are usually used by people who are in a job and for some reason or other want to move. Getting possible interview exposure this way eliminates the risk of having their present employer discover that they are looking for a job. From the replies, they are able to sort out and eliminate the names of those companies with whom they dare not pursue an interview.

Advertising under these circumstances is a time-consuming affair. It is like fishing in the middle of the lake and hoping some fish will see your bait. I suppose that is why so many frustrated people are locked in their jobs. They want to get out but can't find the courage and lack the know-how to take the first positive step.

Over the years my experience, in looking on as people tried using "Help Wanted" ads, or classified and display advertising, has been that the results have been too poor to warrant their use. Who do you suppose is most likely to spot your ad in the paper in case you did advertise? My guess is that it would be the personnel director or one of his assistants. If you did get called in, who do you think would be the person most likely to interview you? My guess again is the personnel director or his assistant. You can be absolutely positive that it will not be the president or any other officer. If you want your interview to be with an officer of a company—and you do, don't expect to get it through inserting a situation-wanted ad.

CHAPTER 6

How to Conduct the Interview

YES, I MEAN THIS. You are to take charge of the interview. This will no doubt sound like heresy to you, for in your previous experience the interviewer will have conducted it. From now on, you will find that you can be in control without the interviewer's realizing it. You have been invited to come in. Your broadcast letter has done a job ahead of you. It has started to create an image of you. It has almost placed you on a pre-sold basis. You are now in an enviable position. You are going in with the dignity of an equal. You have been invited. Even the secretary is expecting you. You no longer have that "hang dog" feeling that you are looking for a job. No, here the job is looking for you. You are no longer just an unemployed person. Your ego is restored. You are the one in a hundred who has been called in—the one who seems to fit their need.

This is not baloney to make you feel good. This is a fact.

The interviewer may have selected you out of 200 or more who sent him letters or who answered his advertisement. Everything you have done up to this point—your résumé, your broadcast letter, your mailing list, your answering of advertisements—has been in preparation for one thing only— getting an interview.

You are now face to face with a prospective buyer of your services. Now he has a chance to size you up, and you, in turn, can take his measure. He has a chance to decide whether or not you are the one his company needs, and you can decide whether or not this is the company for you.

Some wag described interviewing as similar to two strange dogs meeting for the first time. They are reserved and cautious as they size each other up; they either bristle or wag their tails. So it is with people. Don't expect that you will like every interviewer or that every interviewer will like you.

Interviews, however, you must have. There is no way to arrive at an offer of a job except through the interview. Yet I find many people who are fearful of the interview. Truly, this is a transitory feeling. Most people have this fear when they face any unknown situation. Perhaps your worst fear is that you may muff a chance. I say, "So what?" Even if you do muff an interview now and then, there are many more ahead. You might actually find yourself with more interview opportunities than you can possibly handle. I have known of some who couldn't accept more than half of their invitations for interviews. You will find each one easier and more rewarding. I have yet to hear of a one who didn't survive and walk out alive after an interview. Some salesmen have this uneasy feeling every time they call on a new customer. Most great actors have such jitters before going on stage the first night; some have the jitters every time the curtain goes up.

Practice Makes Perfect

Interviews can and will become fun. I have had many people tell me that they look back upon the time when they were interviewing around town as one of the most satisfying and valuable periods in their lives.

If you go about it in the right way, you can control the interview. To do this, however, takes practice. It takes experience to polish the skills you need to handle and control each interview to your advantage. Don't for a minute believe the old saw, "Salesmen are born and not made." Quite the opposite is true. Most good salesmen are made through training and experience. Good interviews require polish, preparation, and, I am sorry to say, a certain number of failures.

An important by-product which will come to you as a result of being interviewed must not be overlooked. Thinking about an interview and working it up properly will stimulate you to remember many of the accomplishments of your past that you had long since forgotten. Once rooted out, these additional selling points must be added to your résumé. Each interview smoothes out your presentation and responses and thus develops in your mind a feeling of adequacy and self-confidence. It also contributes to the storehouse of personal assets you can use at a later date. I strongly urge you then to *grasp every possible opportunity for any interview* that you can get in your job field. Many people hesitate to follow up a job lead because they don't want to put themselves in the position of seeming to ask for something. They will explain to me that they are afraid they are too old or that they are too young, that the job may not pay enough, or that they fear they will have to travel too much. By not accepting each available interview, they are losing invaluable experience.

Make it a rule to take every interview you can get—that's the rule. This is the only way you can acquire practice in the asking and answering of questions and in methods of controlling conversations to your own interests.

No one plays a good game of baseball or makes a good speech without many hours or even months of practice. When you return home after an interview, review it thoroughly in your mind, try to discover where you bungled it and how you could have improved it. Go over and over the whole episode until you have it all clarified to your own satisfaction.

Follow these guidelines. Then, when you come to the interview for the one job you would really give your eyeteeth to get, you will be prepared. You will be able to handle yourself with poise and skill, and you will find yourself completely relaxed. Remember you may get just one chance at this crucial interview; there are seldom any repeats of the truly fine opportunities in life. It is up to you to make the most of this one.

A company president once told me about an experience he had when interviewing a man for the position of company controller. "The man walked in erectly, shook hands firmly, smiled when he introduced himself, and seemed perfectly at ease. However, when I started to ask him questions, he stammered and fumbled, his face reddened and he began to perspire so profusely that his collar wilted. I felt so sorry for the poor man that I opened the window even though the room was cool." Here was a waste of a good opportunity— a waste that could have been avoided if this man had previously taken interview after interview and had had more practice.

Try for a Win

If you are really nervous, pretend to yourself that you are playing a game of questions and answers. It is your role in the game to impress the person who has the job and get that person to offer it to you. Play the game with as free and easy a manner as possible. Try to think of it as just a game; in this way, you will have nothing to lose, and you will find yourself completely relaxed.

At the same time, you must realize that to get the most out of this game you must play it properly; you must try for a win. Genuinely try to get the interviewer to offer you the job. Make him feel that he works for a good company and that you are discussing a good job with many opportunities. Look him in the eye and smile. Do not take your eyes off him. Many job offers are lost because of diffidence. The interviewer is only too likely to interpret diffidence as indifference or uncertainty. This may lead to his doubting your sincere desire to get the job or your ability to do well in it.

This little episode illustrates what I mean. A young man was recently interviewed by a college entrance officer. He wanted very much to get into a certain top school. His high-school record was excellent. When the boy was interviewed, however, he flunked his chance. The interviewer reported that the boy was not at all enthusiastic, that he seemed to have no purpose, and that he seemed not sure that he wanted this particular school. He muffed this interview because of his diffidence.

Go into every interview with determination and enthusiasm. Let the interviewer feel that he has a company to be proud of, even if you do not say it in so many words. Let him see that you admire his company, are enthusiastic about its future, and are eager for the job.

If you do get an offer, don't make a decision at this time. It's a wonderful feeling to know that you are wanted, that you have a choice to make, and that you are in a position to turn down a job. After a few such interviews, you will look forward to the next one. You should have enough confidence in yourself now to leave your résumé at home. Do not take either a briefcase or an attaché case with you. If you do, the interviewer will think you have a résumé in there, and his mind will be on it instead of on you.

Get the Interviewer to Do Most of the Talking

In general, the less you talk and the more you encourage the interviewer, the better the interview will go from your point of view. Force yourself to ask short, pertinent, and informed questions. While the interviewer is answering your questions, get ready to follow his lead and add something appropriate about your own accomplishments and experience. Then ask him another question—and another.

What Kind of Questions Do You Ask?

You will want to know what kind of questions you should ask. First of all, do not make them either subjective or personal. To help you steer and keep in charge of the interview, you should ask questions about the man's business and his interests. Remember, the interviewer is not interested in what he or his company can do for you. He wants to know what you can do for them. Don't ask him about pension systems, annual bonuses, hospital benefits, vacations, holidays, travel problems, or about the possibility of your having to move. *Nothing* will make a prospective employer lose interest in you faster than having to hear questions like these. When your interviewer is sold on you, he will begin to embellish the job, and then he will tell you voluntarily all about the fringe benefits his company provides. When you have him truly interested in you, he will try to sell you on how wonderful his company is. He is now more anxious to get you than you are to work for him; thus, he will tell you all about the extra benefits, and you can discuss them with him.

Use a Loose-Leaf Notebook

It is easy to keep your questions in line if you will do a little homework about the company and the man who is to interview you. The men who have become the most skillful interviewers keep notes on each company and some of its executives in a small loose-leaf notebook. They carry a notebook of only one company at a time. This is to prevent fumbling. It also makes the interviewer feel that you are concerned only with his company. If you have several interviews for one day, carry several notebooks. Leave at home in your file the notes on companies previously interviewed.

Your notes must be in line with your job direction. If this should be in sales, you will probably have notes on total sales, profit per sales dollar, advertising budget and agency, and new products. If your bent is toward finance, you will have notes on capitalization, kinds of stock outstanding, mortgages, bonded debts, preferred stock, profits, depreciation, and cash flow. You will include write-offs, research dollars, new products, new capital outlay requirements, and sources of new capital.

Thus, as the job-hunter asks a question, he pulls out his notebook and says, "Let me see now—do you mind if I refresh my memory? Your sales were up $100,000 a year ago and up another $150,000 this year. How did you achieve such a good increase?" "Isn't this a better percentage than your competitors?" Or "How do these sales compare with those of your competitors?" Any relevant question will do. Using notes always makes a tremendous impression. Interviewers have often commented favorably about it. Again, this job-hunter has used a device to make him stand out as that one man in a hundred.

Stay in the Groove

Confine your questions as much as possible to your specialty. Stay in your job groove. Keep on asking questions, even though you may know the answers. Your job is to get the interviewer to do most of the talking. In doing so, he will sooner or later reveal the problem or problems which are facing him at the moment. Often he will blurt out, "I'll tell you why I called you in. I liked your letter and a certain paragraph made me feel that you might be the man we want."

Now keep drawing him out about his problems. If you are in sales, question him about his selling organization; ask if he sells directly to retail outlets, or whether he uses distributors, wholesalers, or jobbers. If he does, ask him how he gets them to concentrate on his product. Ask whether he has a warehouse at a strategic place and how he keeps his inventories in line with his sales. Ask him how he accomplishes market and sales planning.

I mention such questions only with the purpose of stimulating you to think up some of your own. Develop your own question outline. You will have no trouble in thinking up many more. Do plenty of homework so you will be well prepared for each future interview.

Do Your Homework

You will want to know now how and where to do your homework. Go to the public library—many of them have business sections. Go to your local banks. Find out which of them have business libraries. Insurance companies, investment trusts, and stock brokers all surround themselves with the information you are seeking. You will be surprised to find how many of them employ one or more librarians. These librarians will be glad to help you if only for the sake of public relations.

Perhaps you can get access to a Dun & Bradstreet report through your bank or through a friend. Sometimes an annual report to stockholders of the corporation is available. Review *Reader's Guide* for magazine articles to get background information on the company and its officers. *Fortune, Forbes, Dunn's Review,* to name a few, carry lead articles about many businesses. If the company is publicly owned, *Standard and Poor's Industrials* or *Moody's* could be very helpful. Check *Poor's Register of Directors* for data on individuals you plan to interview. You may find something in *Who's Who.* You will no doubt run across other sources.

When you selected names for your direct-mail campaign, I suggested that you should not be too choosey or selective in picking them. Aside from limiting them as to the size of the company or industry, you would be wasting time being too selective. When you have been requested to come in for an interview, you can then look up everything you can find about the company and its officers. If you do it this way, you simplify the task, for then you need to research only those companies which have shown an interest in you.

Your homework should develop good background material on the company you plan to visit. It will enable you to work up questions which will help you to impress the interviewer with your interest and knowledge about both his job and his company. Don't try to sell yourself; don't try to sell an idea. Don't try to tell him what you can do for his company. The interviewer will consider it preposterous for an outsider with no knowledge of the inner workings of the company to tell him what he can do for it. If your questions are right, they alone will make him think you are smart.

Develop an Outline

Develop an interview questionnaire or outline. This could be made up of the important characteristics of the industry, the company, and the job. If you prepare this correctly, you will develop more and better questions with each successive interview. Try to ask questions which lead up to your own experience and accomplishments. Thus, you try to guide him into retaining the proper job image of you. Try to think through your résumé before you go for your interview. This will help you bring out your strongest points. It will give you more poise and make you more alert during the interview.

The outline will help you not only with the interview but it will also be a great aid afterward when you want to make notes for your record. In further interviews you will then know what ground was covered. Thus, it will help to prepare you for subsequent interviews. Since you may have two or more interviews going simultaneously with different companies, this will be of great help. This is one more reason why you will find the loose-leaf notebooks so useful. By recording the information in the notebook immediately, you can make note of the questions you asked and of your answers to his questions. This will highlight both his interests and his needs. In your next interview you will then be able to concentrate on your fitness for the position.

The Résumé in the Interview

For many years I have suggested that applicants go into an interview without their résumés. I discovered this quite by chance after listening to many individuals giving me all the details about their interviews. Remember, very few executives know how to interview, and they may well be as apprehensive as you. To show executives how to interview, a management firm has put out a booklet called "Comments on Interviewing." This booklet is made up of nearly twenty single-spaced typewritten pages. Some of the titles are "Purpose of the Interview," "Kinds of Questions to Ask," etc., etc. Just to read it is confusing. To use it properly an executive would have to practice hundreds of interviews. I am willing to gamble that not one businessperson in a thousand would ever at.empt to familiarize himself with this book enough to make it of value to him. You can be of tremendous help if you guide the interview into the right channels.

I remember a very shy young man, not at all loquacious, going in for an interview about a job as assistant to the controller of a well-known drug and chemical manufacturer. I had suggested that he withhold his résumé and, instead, just ask questions. The first thing that the controller asked was "Have you brought a résumé?" The man answered that he had and would leave it with him after the interview. The controller insisted on seeing it at once, so my friend handed it to him reluctantly. As the controller put on his glasses and opened it up, the applicant for the job asked him a pertinent question about the company's accounting system. The controller looked up, took off his glasses, laid them on top of the résumé, and from there on, the interview lasted for two whole hours of questions and answers. Not once did the controller open the résumé again.

This illustration shows that the controller didn't need the résumé at all. He asked for it as a matter of habit. He was using the résumé as a crutch. Once a question was thrown to him, he was in his element and could talk with ease and enthusiasm.

After hearing of many, many interviews like this, I concluded that very few executives know how to interview. They are just as nervous and tongue-tied as the applicant. Trade and management associations have written reams and reams of treatises for executives on how to conduct an interview, what questions to ask, etc. If all executives knew how to interview, these instructions would hardly be necessary. Asking questions helps the interviewer; it puts him on familiar ground. There is no subject about which he is better informed and none he can talk about with more enthusiasm than his own job. While he talks, you should think of further questions which will help guide the interview into your field of accomplishment. Your homework will have laid the foundation for all this.

If you are asked point-blank for a résumé, tell him (the truth) that you have one prepared but it is very general and not specific enough. However, you would like to bring in a special one after you have explored the nature of tle job, both its requirements and its problems. Tell him that you can have it ready within the next few days. The interview itself will give you plenty of clues about the problems and direction and scope of the job. Your own questions and his answers will tell you what your résumé should contain. When you come again, you can bring him a résumé which is sharp and points directly to the job. You will then stand out as the person with the special talents they need for this position. This way of presenting the résumé has worked out well in all cases. With a little practice, neither you nor the interviewer will miss the usual generalized or functional résumé.

The Salary Question

I am repeatedly asked for advice on the question of salary. Indeed, it is one of the most difficult of all the hurdles that must be overcome in signing up for a new job. Here are some guidelines.

Some of the first questions tossed to you, and sometimes the very first, are questions like these: "What salary did you make in your last job?" "What salary are you thinking of?" "What salary do you require?" "What salary do you have in mind?"

You must be ready to field these questions and any variation of them. Defer, if you possibly can, all talk of salary until you have presented your case to the best of your ability. Here are some suggestions for answers:

"It's not just a question of what I want but what I am worth to you. I think I will leave that open to your own sense of fairness."

"Your salary for this job may have quite a price range. I, too, have no fixed amount in mind. I am open to negotiation.

Perhaps, after we have discussed your needs and my experience in solving similar problems, we will both have a better idea of salary, don't you agree?"

"I would rather not talk at this time about salary even though it is important—I need to eat. But isn't it more important right now to delve into the job requirements?"

"May we leave that until later? There are many things as interesting to me as salary, such as the place and people I would work with. I would like the feeling of growing with a company. I would like to take on an assignment which no one else wants, and then reap the reward by a raise in salary and possibly a stock option. There are some companies that I wouldn't work for at double the amount I was making, and there might be one that I would go to for less."

Let me mention right here that I am fully conscious of the fact that to many people, success is equated with a high salary. This does not by any means signify that I give this concept my total approval. There are people who get their satisfaction from other things besides money.

You will have no problem about salary in a company which has an organization chart where the job description has been formalized. It will list the duties and responsibilities. The salary range will be predetermined. You will also find out from the chart to whom you report and who reports to you.

In a company which does not have salary structures representing careful appraisal and job evaluation (it is surprising how many good companies lack this), you will have to dig out this information yourself in the interview. You do this by gently exploring the problem and the job assignment, trying to make it all more definite. Get your duties and responsibilities agreed on verbally and, if possible, in writing.

After the job description has been agreed on, the salary can be set. If the job is described properly, the price tag can be more easily and fairly determined. Don't fix your salary too low. This may lose you an opportunity for a good salary when the interviewer had expected to pay more. Don't price yourself out of a job by putting too high a price tag on yourself. Salary should compensate for the job responsibilities and the work to be accomplished. It will differ according to various factors; that is, the size of the company or the geographical area. The level of salaries varies from company to company, even in the same industry. Often salaries are lower in the new glamour companies. They have applicants by the score and so are in a buyer's market. Then, again, some old-established companies may offer you security in lieu of a higher salary.

Sometimes you will be offered the job of someone who is about to retire. You are to go in as an understudy and will be offered less pay than he was getting. In this case, tell the interviewer that you would prefer that the question of salary be deferred for a while. Tell him you would hesitate to accept a salary out of line with that of the other employees, and you would like first to show him what contribution you can make to the company.

A Word of Caution

Sometime you may run up against a situation where the need for your service is so great that the company will pay almost anything you might ask. They may need you badly to solve a specific problem and do not have the right one to do it. For instance, they may have acquired another company through a merger. They need someone to integrate the two, to close up plants, and to dispose of machinery. They may need someone for the really nasty job of firing the old employees. You may be competent in doing an excellent job for them, but where will it lead? You, too, will be let out. You were hired to do a very special job, and when that job is finished you may be, too.

Always be cautious when you are offered an astronomical salary. Weigh all the facts coldly and try to discover what hidden meaning there is to this. Too often a person who needs a position rather desperately will let this fact tip the scales in favor of his accepting a job which he should turn down. The applicant might get so wrapped up in selling himself that he may neglect to analyze the situation.

One very important question which the job-hunter should always ask himself is "Are the people I am going to be working for my kind of people?" I mean morally and ethically, not ethnically. Much of your happiness and your family's will depend on the answer to this question.

When the job and salary are both cinched, do not ask for frosting on the cake. Recently, B. A. had a very successful interview for the position of assistant controller. The controller (interviewer) felt that the salary and duties had been fully decided upon and asked B. A. to see the personnel man to get himself formally on the payroll. When the applicant told the personnel man that his salary was to be $25,000, that individual said that that was more than he got and he had been with the company for ten years. This caused B. A. to get into a discussion as to what he could expect in salary increases in the future and to ask for more details about the job. The personnel man reached for the phone, called the controller and told him that B. A. wanted more information about his salary and duties. The controller answered bluntly that he thought he had outlined all of them very clearly and asked to have the employment held up, saying he would give it more consideration. That was the end of the job.

You may run into a similar situation. A jealous person can undo you in a matter of minutes. Don't give him a chance.

Another man was asked about his family, the number of children he had, and what schools they attended. He told the interviewer that he had four children and added proudly that they were all in private school. The employer then remarked that that must be costing him plenty, and wondered aloud how he could possibly afford that on the salary in question. When he was told that the applicant had independent means, the interview cooled quite perceptibly. A few days later he received a note from the prospective employer explaining that he was not filling the position immediately.

Never mention that you have independent means or intimate that salary is not important. Keep that out of the salary discussion. Employers want hungry people.

Never reveal the state of your finances. If you are up against it, some employer might take advantage of you and offer you less. If you have money, he may feel that the job is not your primary consideration.

Avoid Telephone Interviews

The telephone requests to come in for an interview during a job campaign may be as many as those that come in by mail. Some firms will try to interview you directly over the telephone. Always avoid this and keep striving for a personal interview. Keep control of the situation by saying that this is not a good time for you to talk and ask if you can come in to see him later. Do not let him put you off by telling you that he will call you. Instead, suggest a definite interview time. Say, "Would you prefer next week to this one?" or "Would Tuesday or Wednesday suit you better?" Never leave it to the interviewer's option to call you. Keep the initiative. If he says he can't see you this week, reply, "May I call you next week? It will be easier for me to call you, for I am not always available by phone. I have quite a few interviews scheduled."

Mary P. tells me that when someone tries to interview her by phone she says, "I am so very sorry but I am unavoidably dashing off at this minute. May I call you tomorrow?"

Mr. C.H. says, "I can't talk very well right now as I have someone here; may I drop in tomorrow or the next day so we can talk freely and in private?"

You will develop your own technique and use your own words, but be *sure* you don't let anyone interview you over the telephone. Remember, an interview must be carried on face to face. This way you don't take the chance of a click of the receiver which may be the end of your opportunity.

References

References, like salaries, should be left until the end of the interview. Do not type them on your résumé. Simply state: "References will be furnished on request."

Try not to give out references until you are in the final stage of negotiation. If you give them out too often, the one who has to answer them will get tired of the whole business. At the beginning he may give careful, thoughtful statements, but at the end he may give only perfunctory answers. If one person gets too many requests for references, he may wonder why you need to see so many people and why it takes you so long to get a job. His confidence in you may slip a bit.

If possible, see all the people you use for a reference. Tell them about your job campaign. Review with each of them the details of your past employment. Show them the factual information you plan to use and ask whether they agree with the correctness of your statements. Change things to suit them if they request you to. Leave them an outline of the points in your résumé that refer to their concern. This will not only help you but it will help them to give proper direction to what you wish them to say about you.

Overcoming Bad References

You must know what to do if you find out that someone is giving you a black eye, or, even worse, damning you with faint praise. You will begin to realize that something is wrong after you seem to have had a perfect interview and you think that you are in, and then you are dropped like a hot potato.

Go right back to your interviewer. Ask him what happened and if something was wrong. Ask him if he received replies from all your references and if not, tell him you will get them for him. Oftentimes, if approached this way, he will come right out and tell you the real reason he lost interest. He may even tell you that one of your references was lukewarm, or worse. You will now have to find out where the bad reference came from, although you may already have guessed, for you will know the circumstances about your having left a certain company.

For instance, C. H. discovered he was getting a bad reference from a man with whom he had been associated in business. When they parted he had to sue his former associate to get the money that was coming to him. He licked the problem this way. Whenever he gave out references, he would say, "You will find my references are all excellent with the exception of one." He would then tell the story of having been associated with this man in business and the sad consequences. In this way, he prepared his prospective employer for the bad reference. It then would not count against him.

Another man, M. M., was getting a very dubious reference. His last employer would write, "When he came to us, he had fabulous references. He did all right with us, but he didn't fit in too well. He wasn't contented where he was." When M. M. discovered what was happening, he would say simply, "The references from my previous employers are excellent, except the last one. I quit after six months because the company had suddenly changed the ground rules. I was to report to Pakistan. In Hong Kong, en route to Pakistan, I was cabled to report to Singapore. I had my wife and a four-month-old baby with me. I had to leave them in Hong Kong because I could get no accommodations for them in Singapore. When it became evident that I could get no accommodations at all for them, I resigned." This recital of the facts completely satisfied the employer. The lesson to be learned from these examples is that if you do get a bad reference, bring it out yourself ahead of time and you will minimize its importance.

Personality Tests—The Great Divide

Just when it seems that you are about to be put on the payroll, you may be told that there is one more hurdle to overcome. You have now come to the Great Divide—known as the psychological test. It is one of the great barriers which keeps the unemployed from being employed. It is said that there are more than a million tests given daily for one purpose or another. These tests keep people out of jobs and often keep them from getting promotions. Before you get on a payroll, you may have to take as many as eight or ten of them.

Banesh Hoffman, in "The Tyranny of Multiple-Choice Tests" in *Harper's Magazine*, has this to say: "Busy executives, especially those who lack confidence in their own judgment, are all too happy to hand over to professional testers the job of deciding who is worthy and who is not." It is apparent from the large number of tests that are given that many executives seem to abrogate the vital selection of their teammates to people who have never had to participate in profit-making decisions in the competitive business world.

You will have no choice about taking these tests, whether you like them or not. Wherever they are required, you will be compelled to take them. Otherwise you will not get on the payroll. Inasmuch as you will have to take them, prepare yourself by doing a little homework. There are a number of books which will assist you: *The Brainwatchers* by Martin L. Gross, published by Random House, and *The Organization Man* by William H. Whyte, published by Simon and Schuster. Both of these can be purchased in paperback editions. There are also two magazine articles, both by Martin L. Gross, "The Hire and Fire Tests—Can You Beat Them?" and "The Brain Pickers Can Cost You Your Job," published in *True* magazine. If you do a little homework on testing, you will at least have some idea of what is expected of you and it will help you take the tests in your stride.

Here is a letter from a friend who took some of these tests:

DEAR CARL:

I have accepted a position with ———. Your efforts and those of the Thursday Night Club resulted in a letter which brought in four job offers, plus several other live possibilities. I certainly appreciate the great help.

As I mentioned to you recently in the ——— Club, I had one experience with psychological testing. I was given a battery of tests which took about six hours to complete. Following this, I had an "informal chat" with the psychologist for about an hour and a half. I came away from the entire experience with these conclusions:

1. Anyone with a knowledge of these tests could influence the results of them substantially.

2. In the post-test interview, the good doctor commented that he saw something interesting in my make-up that he would comment on even though he wasn't supposed to. Believe me, he was way off base. From that point on, I felt that I was in the presence of a tea-leaf reader. He would make a rather leading statement, and then wait to see if I showed agreement, confusion, etc.

3. The final step was the most interesting. He mentioned that I had tremendous latent talent ability which if completely unlocked could lead me to undreamed-of heights. He then suggested to me that although he might not be able to take me on, he could lead me to someone who could be of tremendous help in a one-hour period a week for about six to eighteen months.

Incidentally, this testing was requested by one of the companies which was interviewing me. It is pathetic to think that management would have to use as a crutch such hocus-pocus.

I will look forward to dropping in occasionally on Thursday night to offer what assistance I can.

Thanks again for your help.

Don'ts on Handling the Interview

1. Do not take your résumé, your briefcase, or even an envelope with you into the first interview. Leave them in the outer office.

2. Do not talk too much. The interviewer should do more than 50 per cent of the talking. You can manage this by asking questions.

3. Do not try to sell yourself. Let the interviewer want to buy you. Let your past performances and accomplishments do the selling for you.

4. Do not try to sell an idea such as telling what you can do for the company and how you would do it.

5. Do not get involved in a discussion of politics, religion, or the personalities in your previous company.

6. Avoid name-dropping. You do not know what reactions it will set up.

7. Never say, or even imply, that you can do *anything*. Stick to the specialty that brought you in; otherwise you will immediately lower your demand and salary value. Go hungry a while longer.

8. Do not lose your temper no matter what the provocation. You will find some small men who will goad you with contemptuous and slurring remarks. Leave their execution to someone else.

9. Do not get involved in an argument. You can't ever win it. The interviewer is both judge and jury. Change the drift of the conversation with another question.

10. Refrain from criticizing the interviewer or pointing out where he is wrong. Showing up the interviewer is fatal only to you. Quoting Lord Chesterfield: "Be wiser than other people if you can, but do not tell them so."

11. Avoid the question of salary until you feel you have made a sale.

12. Do not let yourself be interviewed over the telephone.
    Do not talk salary over the telephone.
    Do not send your résumé after a request by telephone.

13. Never name your references or allow them to be contacted until you and the prospective employer have had a meeting of minds.

14. Do not write a trite or flowery "thank you" letter in gratitude for the interview. Leave gratitude to beggars. Review, instead, the highlights of the interview. Bring up any additional pertinent points to the interviewer, particularly those that relate to solving his problem. Give him more bait.

CHAPTER 7

Looking for a Job in Secret

TIME AND AGAIN I have been confronted by people who say, "But my problem is quite different," or "I have a real problem. I am employed. I want to get a different job, but I don't dare let my boss know I am looking," or "How do I go about looking for a job without imperiling my present position? If the company finds out that I am looking, I will be fired. This I can't afford. I have very little money and my family needs to eat."

I am forced to tell these people that there is no way in the world to look for a new job and *guarantee* that it can be kept secret. Nothing is absolutely foolproof. You take a risk in everything you do. You can, however, minimize the risk in a number of ways, always with the hope that if you are found out you will be so far along in your job campaign that it will make no difference.

These are some of the ways people use in trying for a better job without jeopardizing their present one:

A. Tell friends they want to make a change.

B. Enroll with an employment agency.

C. Place advertisements in newspapers. This is costly and time-consuming. You may get a dozen or more answers, but they may come from all kinds of people. Too few of them will be from actual employers. Many will come in from individuals who want to sell you something or want you to make an investment in their business. If you are called in as a result of an ad, it will be by the personnel manager and you will have to talk to him and not to an officer. This is seldom to your advantage. If an officer should see your ad, it would be quite by accident.

D. Register with school and alumni placement departments. These usually ask you to forward a résumé which they, in turn, mail out to prospective employers. Do not permit these to be mailed out unless you have been consulted in advance about the list. Your résumé might be sent to your own employer.

E. Get in touch with executive search firms (or consultants). Instead of going to a recruiter at the beginning of a job campaign, concentrate on answering ads and writing letters, both on a third-party basis. Your chances of getting a job through recruiters are extremely small. *Fortune* magazine, in an article entitled "How Executives Get Jobs," has this to say: "Consultants estimate that fewer than one per cent of the men who approach there are eventually placed in client's firms." This figures out to 1 in 100.

F. Answer ads. This, if done under your own name, is extremely dangerous. It can get you in serious trouble since you do not know the recipient; it may be your own company.

Answering ads the third-party way can be extremely effective. I have answered advertisements for many individuals using the third-party approach. They were overwhelmingly successful. Here are some of the letters I sent out:

DEAR SIR:

As Chairman of the Alumni Placement Committee of Harvard Business School, I am writing to you in regard to the position of Vice President of Marketing which is advertised in the February 16 issue of *The New York Times.*

I know an individual whose business experience and accomplishments qualify her for this position. For obvious reasons, she would rather not have her identity revealed until she knows who you are and has more information regarding the advertised position.

If you are interested in pursuing this further, I may be reached at RE 2–7878 or, if you prefer, you may write me at the above address.

Very truly yours,
CARL BOLL

I used this letter in answering four blind ads for this woman. I received three telephone calls and one letter, a 100-per-cent return. My job-seeking friend got four interviews. She now is vice-president of sales for a well-known national organization.

For another person, also on a confidential search, I answered the following advertisement:

DIRECTOR OF MARKETING

Four functions required:
1. Successful food sales, heavy supervisory experience.
2. Home office experience in planning, marketing, administration, and organization building.

3. Experience in meeting continuous sales targets.
4. Chain Headquarters contacts.

The rest of the advertisement told about salary, bonuses, advancement, etc. It was signed by a national firm. Here is my letter:

DEAR SIR:

Your advertisement in *The Wall Street Journal* interested me. As Chairman of the Alumni Placement Committee of Harvard Business School, I know a prospect who measures up to all the requirements listed in your advertisement. I would like to put you in touch with him. He presently is a successful Field Sales Manager for a grocery manufacturer whose products have 100% national distribution.

For reasons you will understand, he prefers to contact you through me.

He has an outstanding record of sales in "problem" markets. He selected and trained both company and brokers' salesmen.

He has succeeded in establishing his company's products in such chains as A&P, Kroeger, Colonial, and Winn Dixie where territory salesmen had failed.

As a member of the Sales and Advertising Committee, he participated in the forming of advertisements for television, magazines, and newspapers.

He prepared market surveys upon which advertising and sales promotion were based.

I shall be pleased to put you in contact with this man. There is no fee or charge for this service.

Very truly yours,

I received an immediate written reply expressing a desire to talk to this man. In a subsequent telephone conversation with the advertiser, I established the fact that he was not the applicant's employer. My friend got the interview. I have a record of 100 per cent answers to my replies to ads.

I have recounted this example to show you how closely I tied this man's accomplishments to the functional requirements of the advertisement. Except for the fact that this is a confidential approach, this follows strictly the outline given in the chapter "How to Get Interviews Through Advertisers." If you can get one reply out of four answers, you will be batting 25 per cent. Even if you don't get this high a percentage of replies, at least you are in there waging an active campaign, instead of sitting around and biting your nails in frustration.

Do not be any more of a burden than you need be to the friends who have agreed to send out letters in your behalf. Get them to supply you with some of their letterheads and envelopes. You can then write the letter which you have agreed on in advance. Mail them copies of the ad and also copies of the letters. They are now prepared to cope with any request. This takes the burden of writing off their shoulders. It benefits you, too, for you are now a free agent to answer any advertisements which seem to fall within your job scope.

Send out third-party letters. This is by far the most effective way to get a job in secret.

Third-Party Letters

Third-party letters can be an effective tool in the secret job campaign, provided they are properly written. Here are paragraphs from two letters written for the same individual, each by a different professional job consultant. Neither was productive of interviews. This is the first:

DEAR SIR:

Can you use a good man in marketing, advertising, promotion market research and intelligent "Public Relations Hidden Selling"?

The man we have in mind is mature, has considerable depth and breadth, and has an outstanding national record dealing with products allied to your field.

His background has been with leading companies and a recognized advertising agency. He knows the teen-age market, the adult market, and the "adult-plus" market.

He has "Mass Sold" and "Specialty Sold" on a national basis.

His appearance, personality, genuineness, and service-mindedness are outstanding. He is a graduate of———University.

May we put you in touch with this man, or answer any questions?

One hundred copies of this letter number one were sent out. Two people asked for information. The result was one interview only—a return of 1 per cent.

Here is the product of the second job consultant:

DEAR SIR:

Locate, evaluate, and create that demand necessary for broader distribution. Modern techniques are the keys to this client's success record.

During the past ten years as VP of Marketing and Advertising, the most effective sales channels were developed and national product-recognition achieved.

In his early 50's, rugged, with plenty of intelligent drive. Married, with two children—fine personal appearance and a personality synonymous with accomplishments.

A strong believer in personal contact in all areas and well-liked by people at all levels. Genuine and thorough, he is a man who works objectively getting the job done right and on time.

May we present the man with the talent for strengthening your sales, profits, and teamwork?

Two hundred and sixty copies of the second letter were mailed to a picked list, resulting in two requests for more information and one for an interview. This is an interview return of less than .4 per cent.

After reading this far, you will have no trouble ascertaining the reason these letters did not pull interviews. Each of them is trying to fashion an image of the applicant merely by using glowing words of evaluation. The letters are vague, trite, and intangible. In the first letter you read, "His appearance, personality, genuineness, and service-mindedness are outstanding." What appeal has that to an employer unless he is looking for a doorman?

The last paragraph in the second letter reads, "May we present the man with the talent for strengthening your sales, profits, and teamwork?" Now this is presumptuous in the extreme. An employer reading this will resent it, and rightly so. He will wonder how this man could possibly know enough about his business to make such an assumption.

When working with a consultant, the job-hunter pays for printing, addressing, and mailing. The letters are mailed by the counselor and the answers come in to him. The counselor gets a fee, depending on the contract, either from him or from the employer. Remember, the pulling power of a letter should be rated not by the answers received but only by the number of interviews secured. Do you realize how costly it is in both time and money to get a return of only 1 per cent from a letter written by someone else, when you could get from 6 to 8 per cent return if you went to work and produced the letter yourself? Many of the third-party letters I have seen over the years should never have been mailed. If you do get a consultant to write it for you, ask that person to show you some samples. If they are anything like the ones I have quoted, pick up your hat and leave.

How to Write a Good Third-Party Letter

If you are already in a job the third-party letter can be a powerful interview getter. Furthermore, it is one of the very few means you have to wage an active job campaign. I used to think that in order to be effective you needed some well-known person such as a lawyer, banker, or a successful businessperson to mail out the letters for you. Recent experience, however, has proved that this is not at all necessary. You can use any friends who are willing to "front" for you. They must be willing to have the answers come to them. They should give only their name and address, but not their telephone number. Otherwise, they may get some calls from people who wish to inquire about you on the phone. Your entire job campaign is predicated on getting personal interviews. Here is a sample letter that pulled:

DEAR SIR:

I am writing to you about a man who, as controller of a $25,-000,000 company, discovered $240,000 of neglected stock. He turned this into a $30,000 profit and thus avoided a loss of $60,000. If your company needs someone in its controller's or financial department, you may wish to talk to this man. I am writing on behalf of this man as a friend. No fee of any kind is involved.

He saved 40 per cent in factory labor expense by initiating company expansion into a low-cost labor area.

Suggested discontinuing 30 unprofitable items, and increased profit 10 per cent as a result.

Organized a 1500-man inventory team which completed taking stock of $6,000,000 in five hours.

Initiated automatic billing, reduced office personnel by five, and still got out bills five days sooner.

Eliminated production delays and faulty deliveries due to lack of raw materials through new inventory controls.

This man graduated with honors from ———— University. He majored in accounting and control.

I will be glad to put you in touch with him for the purpose of a personal interview.

Very truly yours,

The job-hunter picked his names from a list of companies each having over $50,000,000 in sales. One hundred twenty letters brought eleven positive responses and six interviews.

The format of this letter follows the letter-writing technique outlined in Chapter 3, "The Broadcast Letter." In recounting the accomplishments, instead of using the first person, he used the third person right through the letter. There is not a single intangible function mentioned here. Instead, he has skillfully turned the functions into measurable deeds, reciting profits and cost reductions. Is it any wonder this letter produced interviews?

CHAPTER *8*

From Government to Industry

ARE YOU ONE OF THE THOUSANDS OF MEN and women now working in government service—in uniform or as a civilian—who wants to move out into the field of business? If you don't know how or where to start to make such a move, let me assure you that you are no more ignorant than 99 per cent of the people who seek a change of job. Perrin Stryker, in his article "How Executives Get Jobs" (*Fortune*), says, "Because very few executives know how to go about selling themselves into a new position, most are likely to spend many dreary months at it—perhaps a year or more." There is no need for you to waste this much time, if you will thoughtfully use common-sense directions in your endeavors.

Everything I have written thus far about job-finding, résumés, letter writing, and so on, applies to government people, except that perhaps you will need to be more conscise and specific than a job-seeker with a private-business background. Read again the directions in preceding chapters on résumés, letter writing, etc.; study them and apply them. Try to relate your government experience to business terms as vividly and concretely as possible. After you have had a few interviews with private companies you will become aware, as I am, of the reluctance of businessmen to hire former government employees. Regrettably, many people think of government employees as persons who have been living and working in an unrealistic world. After you have had a few interviews with businessmen, some of the following statements may not come as a surprise to you:

"I concede that you have had wonderful experience, but you did that in government. Business is different. I can't envision where we could use you."

". . . we feel that you have some very good experience; but, unfortunately, the years that you spent on a government payroll have resulted in such a loss of time and training for our purpose that we cannot consider you for a position with our company."

"Thank you for coming in to see us. I am sorry to tell you we make it a policy not to bring into our organization people with government experience."

"Your job with the government was nonprofit, so we do not feel that government service is as good as experience gained in private enterprise."

"Sure, you bossed and commanded a whole army, but weren't they under military compulsion? They either did what you ordered them to do or they went to the brig or guardhouse. I'll admit that you were accountable for tremendous capital investments in plants, ships, bases, and shore installations. However, you were not over the barrel as a business manager to make profits for the stockholders. You did not have to make the invested capital pay interest or pay off indebtedness. Nor did you need to create the capital for

newer and more efficient facilities in order to overcome depreciation and obsolescence, or meet the ever-changing competition of
free enterprise. When you needed new facilities, you just junked
the old ones, then called on the taxpayers and us businessmen to
furnish tax dollars out of our earnings."

Colonel R. reported verbatim the following remarks from a
conversation with an executive recruiter of personnel:

"Except for the aerospace and other defense industries, you are
not merchandisable to private industry by virtue of your military
training or accomplishments, although they are definitely impres-
sive. You must possess special skills needed by the companies at
the time, or you must rank so high that the company feels you
will be able to increase its business with government agencies as
a result of this influence."

". . . There is no profit motive in the military. You spend the
funds that are appropriated."

"A military man is considered by some as an individual lacking in
imagination, flexibility, or willingness to make deals."

"Being in charge of a military post is different from motivating
civilians in private industry. The rank and grade structure in the
military establishes authority very clearly. Subordinates are afraid
to dispute it. Not so in a company, especially if the workers are
represented by a union. Giving orders does not guarantee that
they will be carried out."

"I am quite familiar with the manner in which the military gets
a job done—just give an order, and the next in rank will see that
it is done, while the top man is playing golf."

These statements may strike you as extreme, but they are
widely held by businessmen. I am simply trying to prepare
you for what you will be up against.

You may well ask, "But what of the generals, admirals,
secretaries and under-secretaries, and officers of lesser rank

who step from government into fabulous jobs?" One does hear often of some of them becoming the president, chairman of the board of directors, executive vice-president, or general manager of a well-known corporation. How did they get their jobs? Well, in most cases, the corporations came to them. The jobs were arranged long before these men left their government positions. It may have happened that an executive had worked closely with the government person on a specific order or wanted that person for the public-relations effect or for the favorable image this person had created for himself in the press over the years.

And sometimes, I suspect, people are brought in from the government because of the influence they might wield in securing government contracts. Others may be brought in for plain window-dressing. In any case, all are brought in for the contribution they are expected to make to the business in one way or another.

When you cite people like General Lucius D. Clay, who went with the Continental Can Company, or General Douglas MacArthur with Remington Rand, or General Rawlings with General Mills, you may be very certain that each one was hired to contribute to the company's profit potential and that none of these corporations took them on purely as a charitable contribution to society. They were expected to earn their salt.

Always keep uppermost in your mind the fact that business exists solely for the purpose of making a profit and that everyone in that business must contribute to that end. Everything in business boils down finally to a profit-and-loss entry —to the dollar sign.

How Can You Find a Place in Private Industry?

Where does all this leave you? Since no one has handpicked you to run, manage, or even to work in his company, it is up to you to get your own job. To switch into industry you will have to go through exactly the same procedures that someone with private business experiences has to go through, but you will have to work harder at it. In your job-hunting campaign, you will have to present your government experience in such a way that private industry will have no doubt that you have a tremendous value to offer. You must make your presentation so attractive that you will be called in for an interview. You must learn to think and speak and language of business, leaving behind you all the idioms, phrases, and terminology so familiar to various branches of government services. You must translate all this into terms the businessman will recognize and understand and appreciate.

The following clipping from the *Register and Defense Times* was brought to me by Commander M., who anticipated retiring from the Navy in six months and was preparing himself for a job campaign. This was advice given and circulated to retiring officers on "How to Find a Job in Industry."

How You Can Find Key Job Contacts

Personal contact is, without question, the most effective technique for uncovering leads to executive opportunities. But tracking down the persons to contact is usually the bigger puzzler for most retirees. Here are tips on finding key contacts:

Your friends in the world of private enterprise will usually be eager to help if you give them the chance. Your contacts in this group should produce many valuable leads.

Private employment officers who specialize in executive placement can refer you directly to suitable openings among their client companies. Usually, a fee is attached if you accept a position through them.

Personnel consultants and executive search specialists are retained (and usually paid for) by client companies to find personnel with executive talent. Most such consultants are experts on executive requirements developing on the local scene. How can you locate them? Just look under "personnel consultants" in the yellow pages of the phone book.

Management consultants frequently uncover major needs for executive talent in their analyses of client companies and also like to be able to recommend personnel to fill such needs. They are usually listed under "engineers-management" or "business and financial consultants" in the telephone directory.

Officials or professional societies and associations operating in the area of your interest can often provide a very good picture of local conditions and needs, and will frequently provide you with valuable contacts in line with your past experience. And, don't forget, this also applies to editors of trade and business publications.

The top personnel of the local chamber of commerce also have their fingers on the pulse of personnel needs. In addition, they can frequently point out new or expanding businesses which may be in need of your talents.

Bank officials can supply much information of the same kind. It is not unusual for them to be on the lookout for executive talent for companies in need of improved administration in order to convert a picture of loss to one of profit, and, incidently, protect the bank's investment.

You should remember that the heads of university business administration departments usually have their hands deep in local business problems and are often asked to recommend suitable talent for position openings. They are glad to come through with much valuable advice.

Personnel officers and executives of companies operating in your area of interest can provide much valuable help—especially if you are not applying for a job with them. And it may happen, as it has before, that it will suddenly dawn on them that you have exactly the ability they need.

Covering these contacts will produce many valuable leads in line with your own experience. Follow them all—even those which may seem off the beam. Each new lead should produce a number of others, provided you take the "whom would you suggest that I see?" approach at some point in your discussion with each man. And, be sure to leave your résumé with every contact you make. With each one left, you will create a small segment of incipient energy which will act to produce leads to opportunities in line with your requirements.

Moreover, you should make liberal use of the names of your contacts as you make the rounds. With each new man, say that John Smith of National Trust (or whoever) suggested that you see him.

I should be sorry for any servicemen who followed the advice given in this article. This approach to job-finding is completely contrary to all my experience. If you were to follow this advice, I believe you would get dizzy on the merry-go-round of courtesy interviews—a costly, time-consuming, and demoralizing ride. Much of the advice in the article is what I call the tin-cup approach or plain panhandling. You are advised in the article to throw yourself on the auction block—a procedure that would undoubtedly lower your prestige and demand value.

No doubt the writer meant well, but my feeling is that he showed scant understanding of what is required in the *execu-*

tive prestige-job market. One wonders whether the author ever tried to find a high-level job himself, using the methods he proposed in the article, or whether the article was written on the basis of a compilation of hints gleaned from many of the impotent books on job-finding found on every library shelf. It may be that his method might be sufficient for a government employee who is looking for *any* job in private industry; it is definitely not sufficient for a high-caliber person who is looking for an executive position that pays a substantial salary.

On the basis of the advice given in the article, the several hundred résumés you send out would probably sooner or later find their way into the file cabinets of personnel directors and executive recruiters instead of on the desk of an important official in a company. A résumé that is filed will seldom do you any good, and often it can do you harm. By themselves, résumés are often too general to sell the individual. They merely emphasize your pitch for a special job. When a personnel director receives a call about you he searches his file. If he finds your résumé there, he will say, "Oh, yes, we have his résumé in our file. He wasn't of any interest to us. If he had been, we would have called him in for an interview before this."

I have known of cases where the job-seeker puts on a second campaign after having learned that he neglected to emphasize in both his letter and his résumé the fact that he was a specialist. Now when he does get an interview, the interviewer has the two résumés in front of him—the first general one and the new one which highlights the man's specialty. It is understandable that he is more than apt to be perplexed and ask about the difference. This is not always easy to explain, and the job-seeker would have been better off had he not bothered to send the first résumé.

I am often asked whether it is advisable to buy the services of a job counselor. My answer is "No." No matter how good he is purported to be or how successful he is touted, my strong feeling is that the task of finding a job that is right for you can best be done only by *you.* The efforts you make toward this end and the experience you gather along the way can only result in plusses for you.

Recently, a Colonel D. came to me for help. He had already explored many of the counseling organizations whose advertising you find in newspapers. In their ads they promise to advise you, write your résumé, and do your mailings for you. Some even promise to get you a job. They offer to help you prepare direct and third-party letters—all for a fee, of course. I reviewed the file of material and all the correspondence that resulted from the colonel's association with one of these firms. True, the firm did arrange for some interviews for him, but he was greatly disappointed with the results of the total operation.

One particular group of job counselors aims its advertising directly at servicemen. One read, "Retiring Officers—Civilian Jobs in the $25,000 to $75,000 Range." You have probably seen this kind of ad yourself. If you are thinking about using an agency of this sort, before you pay out any money or sign a contract, I beg you to ask them first to furnish you with the names and addresses of ten people whom they have placed. Then make your own investigation from this list.

Another thing—don't be talked into buying a mailing list from anyone, even if according to the sales pitch the list includes the choice firms in American industry. It was found that one so-called "Valuable List" contained the names of *six* men in the same company. Imagine these six men comparing notes after having received the same letter from you! I say, make up your own list. It's not easy to do, but I firmly believe that it will be time and energy well invested in order to get the exposure for the job you want.

I feel strongly that you should do *everything* in connection with your job-hunting yourself. There is no other way you can make your résumé effective, come up with a strong, convincing letter, and be prepared for a good interview. You need to go through these processes yourself to tone up your belief in yourself. It makes no more sense to have someone else do this job for you than it does to have someone do your physical fitness exercises for you.

Now, let's go back a little. Reread Chapter 2 on résumé writing until you get the whole significance of it. Use common sense—try to be objective about your would-be employer and try to understand his problems. If you were the employer, what would you want an applicant to offer before you would consider him or her? Smother all feelings of your own problems at this stage of the game.

Develop your résumé as a salesman develops his samples. Remember, this is your merchandise, your bag of saleable items. Recall how a door-to-door brush salesman may pull out one brush to gain entry into a house. Once inside, he makes it his business to determine as quickly as possible what he has that this particular customer may need. He will have a great number of items he can show, but it has been proven that he seldom needs to show more than 5 percent of his wares. The trick is in knowing *which* 5 per cent of his total stock he has to use to make the sale.

Tailor your résumé for the civilian market. Avoid terms

familiar mainly to the military, such as logistics, basic planning, strategic and tactical capabilities. Translate such terms into specific and simple language. Highlight accomplishments in functional areas in terms used by civilians to measure performance, progress, or scope of responsibility.

The first draft of your résumé may be only one paragraph. As you keep working on it, it will grow to two or three paragraphs, and eventually to several pages. However, in your first draft it is important that you write down each thought as it occurs to you. Start to list various functions you have performed, then add the actual accomplishments to your credit within these functions. Functions alone are mere abstractions. You need to use them to create a picture of how effective you were in a particular capacity; so think of the action that that function led to, or the problem it may have solved. Be specific, giving numerical statements as to size, dimension, or measurement. For instance, if you worked in a Navy shipyard, was the work behind schedule when you took over? How many months was it behind, and how quickly did you bring it up to current on repairs and new construction? Were you able to do this with the same work force or with a reduced one? State figures in numbers or percentages of the total.

Or suppose you had been working at an Army air base. Did you find planes on the ground for lack of repair parts and proper maintenance? Was there an overabundance of some parts and a shortage of others? How quickly did you bring the inventory into balance? Were you able to cut the total inventory and still provide an efficient operation?

I recall the story of an Army captain who had been assigned to a depot in Indiana. He found warehouses filled with supplies ordered for the Spanish-American War and for

World War I. He found saddles and equipment for thousands of horses and mules. He got permission to "clean house," and he did it with a vengeance, thereby releasing badly needed warehouse space. Had he not accomplished this, it would have been necessary to have found new warehouse space—a costly capital investment. He saw a job that had to be done and did it, even though others before him hadn't dared to tackle it.

If you have ever reorganized anything, cite in your résumé draft how much money you saved the government, how much manpower.

Here are some other examples that may help you:

Colonel Barbara B.: "I reorganized civilian personnel to handle an increase of 200 workers.

"I saved 1030 man hours, developed standard yardsticks and workload ratios."

Major Lewis W.: "I reduced inventory supplies by 33 per cent through the use of IBM control checks on personnel at bases.

"I cut fuel and food consumption 5 per cent by setting up standards.

"I saved $6,000,000 per year through centralized garaging and terminating unnecessary garage leases."

Are you beginning to see how these people developed strong saleable specialties? As you write your draft, translating function into deeds, you will begin to see (and maybe it will surprise even you) how your own specialties will emerge. You may find that you have accomplishments that could be categorized into the fields of finance, methods and procedures, accounting, manufacturing, building and equipment maintenance, or public relations, to mention a few. If you find that there are several directions in which you can go, it is wise to *develop and concentrate on only one at a time.* Prepare separate résumés, if necessary, to present to prospective employers, so that your specialty will appeal particularly to him and his needs.

I will give you parts of two different résumés prepared by one Navy officer in the following paragraphs. Notice how ineffective the first one is because he simply lists the functions he performed. Then, in the second, mark how he turned each function into a concrete accomplishment with a numerical measurement. Is there any question which of these would sell him as a decision-making, profit-conscious business manager?

This is the first résumé prepared:

Duties and Responsibilities—General Scope

Direction and control of all cost inspection activities in the Eastern area encompassing the Eastern seaboard. Directed the operations of 30 branch and resident offices employing a staff totaling 400 accountants, clerks, and 30 Navy officers.

Responsibility for assuming and maintaining audit control over all Army, Navy, and Air Force contracts assigned to Navy for audit cognizance in the area. Contractwise the area had at the height of defense activity 3,000 contracts under audit totaling $6,000,000,000 distributed among 1,000 contractors engaged in all forms of industrial activity.

Specific Duties

1. Determination of financial responsibility of prospective suppliers to perform contractually prior to completion of negotiations and award of contract.
2. Survey internal controls and accounting systems to determine the adequacy and dependability of the system of internal control and accounting procedures.
3. Recommend changes in contractors' accounting systems where

systems are not practically adapted to cost determinations as required on the basic contracts.

4. Conduct initial pricing studies as required by Contracting Bureaus prior to negotiation of contracts.

5. Preparation of advisory reports on fixed price contracts containing redetermination clauses and submit recommendations regarding final price under the contract.

6. Audit of costs incurred under cost-plus-fixed-fee contracts to determine allowability under government regulations and the terms of the specific contract.

7. Determination of fixed overhead rates for inclusion in cost-plus-fixed-fee contracts.

8. Audit of proposals submitted by contractors under terminated contracts.

9. Conduct special investigations or studies as requested by higher authority. Examples of the scope of these special investigations and studies include:

   a. Analysis of Navy cost of manufacturing products which can be procured commercially.

   b. Analyzing comparative cost data submitted by various contractors on a competitive basis within a specific industry.

   c. Special investigations for fraud or other irregular practices.

   d. Analyzing contractors' financial condition and recommending various forms of government or private financing to maintain production of vital supplies.

   e. Studies of contractors' costing practices and procedures to determine the equity and reasonableness of costs eventually charged to government contracts.

The position of Supervisory Cost Inspector in the Eastern Area requires that the incumbent possess a sound knowledge of all phases of accounting and auditing. I have all these background requirements.

Here is the revised résumé of the same man:

REGIONAL DIRECTOR, COST INSPECTION SERVICE, NAVY DEPT., NEW YORK.

As Regional Director, I administered the audit of 3,000 Defense Department contracts totaling $6,000,000,000, distributed among 1,000 contractors engaged in all forms of industrial activity.

Managed the operations of 3 Branch and Resident offices employing a staff totaling 400 accountants and auditors.

Directed an organization that effected savings to the government amounting to $60,000,000 annually.

Revised the scope of audit under industrial contracts resulting in an 80% reduction in Navy audit personnel. I reduced the cost of area operation 70%.

Developed the original pattern for the Defense Department's coordinated concept of audit. On a nationwide basis, the coordinated plan of audit reduces by as much as 60% the number of personnel required to conduct audits at 600 locations.

Conducted reviews of contract pricing proposals and effected downward revision of prices in 60% of the cases studied.

Recommended revisions to industrial concerns' auditing systems and systems of internal control where they were inadequate for performance of government contracts.

Conducted studies of all forms of industrial cost systems to determine the equity and reasonableness of charges to government contracts.

Initiated and completed special investigations for fraud and irregular practices which have resulted in several Federal Court actions. I analyzed contractors' financial conditions and recommended government or private financing.

Conducted comparative studies of Navy versus Industry costs in the manufacture of clothing, paint, rope, and electrical fittings. Many Navy shops were closed because the study showed that industry could do the job more economically.

Assisted in the drafting and editing of "Armed Services Procurement Regulations—Contract Cost Principals."

Arranged with five national public accounting firms the first practical training course for Naval Officer personnel. This consisted of
actual experience in clients' offices.

You will be interested to know that this last version of his
résumé "grooved" him in a straight line for a controllership,
and that is exactly where he landed—with a large Eastern
corporation.

Your Mailing List

Make up your own list of companies and presidents as suggested in the previous chapter. *Do not write to anyone but
the president.* He will call you in and see you himself or ask
someone else to see you.

Your choice of names of companies depends on your individual decision as to whether you want to work for a large or
a small company. Remember to keep track of all your returns
and evaluate them for future mailings. Your experience and
specialization may determine whether you select a large or
small company and you will, of course, keep in mind the fact
that a small company cannot afford a large computer if
E.D.P. is your specialty.

Your Broadcast Letter

Follow the directions previously given in the chapter on
"The Broadcast Letter." They apply as well to government
employees as to private businessmen. *First*, write your broadcast letter using your carefully prepared résumé. At this stage
of job-hunting do not waste time, money, or morale on any
other thing. Write and rewrite your letter—even if you have

to rewrite it twenty times before you are satisfied. You can use the samples given in earlier pages to help you develop the "style" of your letter. Develop short, effective paragraphs. Use the pronoun "I" as often as you wish; don't worry about sounding immodest. Your letter is about *you*, and your reader wants to know about you.

If you have achieved unusual results in any capacity, take credit for them. Should you find yourself hiding your light under a bushel basket, remember that you were the person responsible for getting that job done, even though you may have had many assistants. If the project had failed, *you* would have been the one who would have gotten the blame.

The following case history of another naval officer will give you a better understanding of what I mean. At no time does he mention in his letter that his experience was military. As his interviews progressed, he found that having been in the Navy was no longer a problem. By this time, the employer was more interested in finding out what he could do in a specific job. His story, just as he gave it to me, shows clearly what I am trying to say and should prove helpful to you.

1. When I decided to retire from the Navy, I had made no preparation for getting a job. I gave the Navy my full required six months' notice with the idea that I would then begin a campaign.

2. I then started to prepare a résumé using the ——— brochure as a guide. It was a great waste of time. I spent at least two hundred hours on the résumé and all I accomplished was to compile a chronological history of what I had done for the last 25 years. The unfortunate thing about it was that I did not list accomplishments.

3. I sent this résumé in three directions. First, I started answering ads in *The New York Times*, submitting my résumé together

with a short covering letter. Out of some twenty such letters, I didn't receive one interview. Some companies sent me a form to fill out.

Second, I sent my résumé to former classmates and friends. This was also a waste of time. I got back a lot of nice letters, but never an interview.

Third, I sent 10 per cent of my résumés to the alumni department of ———— school. I got no contract through the school, although I spent many hours, carefully following the school's directions, putting the résumés in backers, filling out forms, etc.

4. After three months, I started attending Carl Boll's Thursday night sessions in New York. Suddenly I awoke to the fact that I didn't really know what kind of a job I wanted and that I had not been telling prospective employers what I could do. I hadn't adequately explained what I had accomplished or what I was interested in. Furthermore, there had been a definite block in my thinking, because until that evening I thought the most important thing I had to say was that I was retiring voluntarily and that all my previous experience had been in the U.S. Navy. Much later I came to realize that employers are much more interested in "What Can You Do for Me?" Through listening to the group and answering questions about what I had been doing, I began to develop a simple one-page letter. This letter changed every week.

My first letter was devoted entirely to what I had been doing in the Navy.

My second letter listed all my accomplishments but did not focus on any one, and I still kept stressing my service in the Navy.

The next letter put all the stress on controllership and purchasing.

The fourth letter focused on distribution, for I had at long last come to the conclusion that my forte was distribution control.

In my final letter I put all the stress on control. I told what I had accomplished and did not mention the Navy at all.

This was the draft of his final letter:

As Director of Control in a large organization, I developed an electronic data control system for order processing. This raised effectiveness to new highs in measured performance.

My experience in controlling, accounting, ordering, purchasing, and inventory systems might be useful to you in your organization. You may be interested in additional examples of what I have done.

I established controls for a hard-goods inventory of 325,000 line items. Improved stock position by 55 per cent without an increase in inventory.

I devised a data card procedure for determining economical order quantities and speeded up purchase operations that saved $10,000 annually.

In a large distribution branch, I cut payroll expense over $80,000 a year by revising control functions in the receiving department.

Developed picking ticket controls used in an automatic warehouse.

I attended ——— University and received an M.A. degree from the ——— Business School in 1953.

I would be pleased to discuss further details of my experience with you in a personal interview.

Sincerely yours,

His case history continues:

All along there had been a tendency on my part to think humbly. I was unwilling to take credit for the work of subordinates reporting to me. I think this came from a military officer's desire to stress the part of subordinates in the work.

I began to prepare a list of companies for which I would like to work and, in the meantime, answered ads with the letters which were improving each week. I began to get scattered interviews. In answering ads, I used only the final letter quoted above. From February 20 to 26, I answered a total of sixteen ads from *The New York Times* and *The Wall Street Journal*. At no time did I include a résumé with my letter.

Those sixteen letters alone resulted in four interviews. In the four interviews, only one company was interested in a résumé. Several companies showed me stacks of résumés and said that they had called me because my approach was so refreshing.

Suddenly, I was no longer faced with the question of getting *a job;* now there was the question of *which job* to accept. Minutes after I agreed to take my present position, an offer just as attractive came in from a firm where I had been interviewed a few days previously. I think I can sum up my experiences in some generalities:

1. You must know what you have accomplished and be able to relate it to others.

2. You must be able to put it in an interesting short letter, which will result in the employer's wanting to talk to you. One page is preferable.

3. You must get interviews; confidence grows with each interview.

4. Filling out employment office forms by mail is a waste of time, since it is a delaying tactic by the company which sends them.

5. Employers really don't care much about age, military service, where you worked, etc.; they just want to know if you can do the job for them.

6. Employers don't have time to screen long résumés, and résumés don't reveal, usually, what a person can do. Furthermore, they aren't going to hire you until they have *seen* you anyway. By employers, I don't mean personnel managers, but the person you will be working for.

Notice how quickly things changed for this ex-Navy officer when he got a good letter in the mail and when he began answering advertisements in the manner described in the chapter "How to Get Interviews Through Advertisers." Note also that 25 per cent of the persons who received these letters requested an interview. This closely approximates my average goal, which is 20 per cent. His earlier letters to advertisements had pulled a zero response. With his new approach, he had a choice of jobs.

There are occasionally times when mentioning military experience is a tactic that works all right. Generally, it is all right for a young man who has just finished school, gone into service, and then begun to look for a job when he has finished his military stint. A young man who wrote the following letter mailed out forty-seven and received twelve requests for interviews. He received a telephone request from the head of a large department-store chain who came to New York a day later to interview him. He got a job offer the same day at a salary three times higher than his previous one and was on the payroll in less than a week. A miracle? Yes, indeed! But he worked it himself. Have faith in yourself and work your own miracle. Here is his letter:

Dear Ms. ————:

I have just been discharged from the United States Navy where I served as an officer, commissioned as a specialist in mass feeding. I supervised the preparation and service of 1,500,000 meals to officers, aviation cadets, and enlisted men.

You may have merchandising and supervisory problems in connection with the operation of your customer and restaurant facilities. If so, my experience and background may be of use to you. During my tour of duty, I performed the following: planned all menus, and purchased foodstuffs, supplies, and equipment. Being familiar with nationally known resources, I reduced food costs to the Navy, saving $1,500,000 in a six-month period. I specialized in setting up menu programs to meet sectional eating habit problems; supervised up to 300 enlisted and civilian personnel.

Prior to entering the service, and since my discharge, I have been employed by the ——— company. I have been completely responsible for the installation and operation of feeding facilities for its 4,000 employees.

During this period, I designed, purchased equipment for, and supervised the installation of a cafeteria and two canteens; hired, trained, and supervised 40 food service employees; planned menus, purchased all foodstuffs and supplies, set up a financial report system and cash control. Despite low selling prices, high food and high labor costs, the food facilities were operated at no cost to management.

In June of 1948, I was graduated from the ——— School of Business Administration. I specialized in Retailing.

I would like an opportunity to discuss with you a more detailed account of experience.

Can you now see from the letters illustrated above why they pull interviews? You too can do what may now seem impossible. Perform your own miracle. *Perform*—that means work at it. Make the advice in this book work for you, as it has for so many others, even though you are a government employee.

CHAPTER *9*

Executive Search Firms and Employment Agencies

Executive Search Firms

EXECUTIVE SEARCH FIRMS are more often referred to as *recruiters*. They are also called by many other names, some complimentary, some not, depending on whose ox has been gored. If a recruiter has lured a key person away from a company, that concern may call the recruiter a pirate. On the other hand, if the same company has gained a good employee, the recruiter will be called a talent scout. So, head-hunter, talent scout, or flesh merchant—the name given to the recruiter will depend entirely on whether or not the speaker has been helped or hurt.

The two questions most often asked me about executive search firms are:

1. Can they be of any help to me?
2. Which one can serve me best?

My answer to Question One is: "Yes, they can be of help to you, provided you are employed. If you are unemployed, you will get very little help from them."

My answer to Question Two is: "It is impossible to single out the ones which will be of most help to you. This will depend on your specialty and on the specialty of the individual search firm. Some of them concentrate on banking and investment, some on business, while others specialize in such fields as marketing, manufacturing, retailing, controlling, or general management."

Business cycles may have considerable bearing on which kind of executives are in demand. During a recession, when cost cutting and profit improvement are a necessity, presidents, financial vice-presidents, controllers, and budget directors are wanted. When production outruns sales, the hue and cry is for marketing experts. When inventories bulge, merchandise controllers and electric data processing experts are in demand. Other times there are calls for help in the fields of manufacturing, purchasing, and industrial relations. These cyclical demands are reflected in the job specifications listed by the search firm. The reception—warm or cool—that the job-seeker gets from the recruiters and employment agencies depends on whether or not he or she has the requirements to fill one of their positions.

Consultant News, Templeton Road, Fitzwilliam, N.H. 03447 has compiled lists of more than 300 search firms and 50 employment agencies. They sell for $5.00.

"Job Finding Rackets—Phoney Counselers Reported Bilking Uncounted Victims" is the title of a recent syndicated article by Sylvia Porter, financial columnist.

"Thousands of executive positions are opening every day . . . if you desire a change, let us study your potential. . . ."

"A $30,000 to $95,000 yearly position could be only a résumé away . . ."

"These," she says, "are typical of the lures being put before young executives by phony 'executive counselors' who promise to find the men dazzling new jobs and to multiply their salaries—but who cannot deliver.

"Masquerading under such sophisticated titles as 'management psychologists,' 'career counselors,' and 'executive search firms,' these pseudo employment agencies are now reported to be bilking uncounted victims out of 'service fees' ranging from $350 to $3,000."

She quotes John Nichols, the manager of the Chicago Better Business Bureau's financial division, as saying, " 'A small group of incompetent promise-makers have infiltrated the industry, leaving a trail of unsatisfied job-seekers behind them.' "

Sylvia Porter goes on to say, "Typically, the career-counseling phony moves into plush quarters, prints up an impressive-appearing array of gimmicky 'career advice' and advertises everything from 'evaluation of career opportunities' to a 'guarantee' of a job paying a five-figure salary.

"One now defunct outfit boasted a 'jet-age system of instant communication that speeds your profile to potential employers within 72 hours.' Another claimed 20 offices, from New York to Hong Kong, and the 'world's most unique and unusual career advancement program.'

"The victim is lured into signing an extravagant contract and paying an exorbitant, non-refundable 'service fee' before any of the contract's provisions have been fulfilled.

"As it turns out, the firm is nothing more than an unqualified, fly-by-night employment agency, operating on a shoestring and without a state license.

"The 'career counselors' simply send sheaves of résumés to dozens of companies—unsolicited. The résumés may or may not result in a job or better salary. The 'counseling' may be next to useless. In the words of one victim, 'The psychological evaluation was a farce. The counseling amounted to bull sessions.' "

The recruiting business has mushroomed in the last few years, so that today there are purported to be some five hundred search firms. This gives you plenty of selection. Do you realize that if you could schedule two interviews a day, ten a week, or forty a month, it would take you two and a half months to see one hundred search firms?

A former financial vice-president decided that because of high salary requirements, recruiters ought to be his best bet. He told me that he spent two months making the rounds at a cost of $2,000 in addition to the loss of time. He did get a number of interviews through them, but not one resulted in a job.

Executive Search Firms Are Hired by Management

Before you go to a recruiting firm, you should have a clear understanding as to its purpose and objectives. These firms are not employment agencies. They work only for corporations seeking executive ability, and they are paid a fee for this service. They have a contract with a specific employer to find a very specific executive. This person may be the very top man of a corporation or a second-echelon executive. The salary offered may range from $25,000 to an unlimited top when the order has been to get *the* man. The recruiter may have told the employer that he would bring in the very best person in the industry, even if he had to search the highways and byways. The specifications will have all been drawn up and usually preclude everyone except someone with a specific industry or functional experience. The person the recruiter is looking for is a successful one in a strong, prosperous firm, most likely a competing one. In order to get such a person, the job offer must be made alluring and challenging, with salary bonuses, titles, and stock options. Sometimes an individual is loath to change unless he is allowed to take with him his own team of trusted assistants. He will often be granted this privilege, so great is the seeming need for his services. It makes little difference that his former company is stripped of key personnel.

Since the recruiter gets a fee for his service based on a percentage of the first year's salary plus out-of-pocket expenses, you can well understand why his obligation is to his client and not to the job-seeker who comes to him off the street or as a courtesy referral from a friend. Most recruiters will grant you an interview, not only out of a sense of courtesy but because it is good public relations. Too, there is also a vague hope that you may be the person they are seeking or that you may be able to suggest a possible candidate.

Recruiters Are Seldom Interested in Men Out of Jobs

The chance that you will be the person selected for a certain job is mighty slim. *The Wall Street Journal* once quoted Hallam B. Cooley, now conducting his own search firm in San Francisco, as saying, "About 99 per cent of the people we get for positions are already employed." Many of the recruiting firms state quite bluntly in the sales brochures which they give out to employers that the people they look for are rarely active job-seekers or unemployed. In spite of this, people looking for jobs swamp the search firms daily with hundreds of telephone calls, visits, letters, and résumés.

Fortune magazine published an article by Perrin Stryker on "How Executives Get Jobs." In this, he tells a great deal about the place of the recruiters in the job market. I recommend it highly. Mr. Stryker interviewed a great many of these firms. He tells about one in New York which claims to have records on 250,000 people. Another claims to have listed 120,000 names. Several others list 50,000 names. I quote Mr. Stryker: "At Booz, Allen & Hamilton, for example, the data about job-seeking executives are carefully transferred to cards according to industry, salary, etc., and when a client asks for a particular kind of executive, the cards are quickly searched for a possible candidate. If the search firm turns up someone who looks good, the consultants begin checking his or her references, subordinates, business contacts, and general record. If these look good, the consultant may put the candidate through a battery of psychological tests before presenting him to a client. Nevertheless, it is the rare executive in the files who gets picked as a candidate." An executive with Booz, Allen & Hamilton says, "Many people let us know that they are available. Frequently, they have either been passed by or are at the top of their companies and don't know where to go from there. The chances are one out of five hundred that we'll need that guy immediately." Mr. Stryker confirms this when he states, "One of the surest ways for an executive to be overlooked as a candidate is to get buried in a consultant's file."

During the thirty years that I have been working with job-seekers, I have established contacts with a great many recruiting firms. My relations with some of them are exceptionally friendly, as I am considered an excellent source of leads for the kind of people they are seeking. I get many telephone calls and letters asking for people with specific talents. When I explain to the recruiter that I have several possible leads for him, he invariably wants to know whether or not they are employed. If I reply in the negative, practically every recruiter loses interest; but they do go on to say, "Don't you have anyone of that description who *is* employed?" My answer to this question is invariably: "No, I do not." I refuse to be party to disturbing someone who is employed. I do not want the responsibility of having pointed out what seemed to be a greener pasture but may turn out in the end not to have been a pasture at all—but a mirage. I equate a job with marriage; one doesn't know definitely whether it will "take" until one is in it. Who am I to tell a person that his or her present marriage would be improved with another spouse? I do not like to disturb someone who is apparently well satisfied with the status quo.

I have received hundreds of job descriptions from the search firms. I pass each one on to people looking for jobs. In all the years that I have done this, only three unemployed people have been placed through recruiters.

I have no fault to find with these firms. They are dedicated people under contract to do a certain job for the people who engage them and who pay the fees. Their job is to search for a candidate. They very rarely place one who comes to them. My concern is to help people find jobs and while they are at it to keep up their morale and self-confidence. Neither morale nor self-confidence can be kept up for long by having a number of empty courtesy interviews. My advice to the job-

seeker is to call on the executive search firms only when there
is a lull in the interview schedule.

Employment Agencies

Do not turn to employment agencies until:

1. You have your broadcast letter going full blast. (This means
   you have already mailed your letters. You will now have ten
   days to two weeks of relatively free time before the interviews begin.)
2. You have cut out all employment agency "Job Openings" in
   the newspapers.

You are now ready to go to the agencies. Do not run
around to them promiscuously. Get in touch only with those
whose advertisements are of interest to you. However, be
sure to include those which advertise jobs that are fairly close
to your specialty, even though there may be divergencies,
such as age, salary, etc. You have nothing to lose by taking a
shot at them. Let the employment agency make the decision
as to whether or not you are suitable for the job. This is a
decision you are not qualified to make. Remember: no job
description or advertisement has ever been written that fits
only one person. Even though you may not have all the de-
sired qualifications, the agency may have been searching a
long, long time and may be quite ready to make certain con-
cessions to fill the job.

The Necessity of a Résumé

A résumé will be a necessity when you call on agencies;
you can't get along without it. This résumé should be pref-
erably one page long and never more than two. Have it

grooved or geared to the particular job you are seeking. Prepare several of these résumés, each pointed in only one direction. You want to sell one specialty at a time, *and one only*.

Getting Agency Interviews

You may either telephone or write to an agency about an advertisement. When you write, adapt your broadcast letter to the advertisement. If your broadcast letter doesn't suit the requirements, refer back to the chapter on "How to Get Interviews Through Advertisers," and the advice given there.

See Agencies in the Afternoon

Do *not* go to the offices of employment agencies in the morning unless you want to stand in line with teen-age typists, file clerks, and office boys while you wait your turn to be "processed" and to fill out the ever-present card. This may undermine your morale.

Herbert Graper, who formerly operated an employment agency and who has recently retired as national personnel director from Dun & Bradstreet, gave this advice: "Never go to an employment agency in the morning. At that time, the agency people are busy interviewing the 'line-up' of applicants and looking over their cards to see whether they are complete. With a long line waiting, there is no time to go very deeply into anyone's record. Go to an agency in the afternoon when the morning interviewing and appointment-making are over. You will then find the agency operator more relaxed and willing to listen. You then have a chance to visit with him about the job opportunity he advertised. You may soon be on such a friendly footing that he will go to great lengths to get you interviews." Always try for an afternoon appointment. If you are asked to come in during the morning, you can always say you are busy; and, indeed, you had better be, if you are looking for that job. Mr. Graper says too: "Don't go to see employment agencies on Mondays. That is the day when they get the rush from the weekend advertising, and time is at a premium."

Which Are the Best Agencies?

I am asked over and over again to recommend a good employment agency. Here I am forced to give the same answer that I gave about executive recruiters. Whether an employment agency or a recruiting firm is good, bad, or indifferent depends entirely on your own personal experience with them. You will like the ones that are friendly and helpful. You will cuss the ones that treat you as a mendicant. You will dislike the ones that tell you that you are too young or too old, too inexperienced, or so experienced that you may be set in your ways. You will be disgusted with those who are as impersonal as a postal clerk selling you stamps.

A few years ago one of the people I was helping decided that while he was making the rounds of employment agencies he would make a one-man census. He resolved to tabulate them as good, bad, or indifferent, basing his opinion purely on personal reaction. He marked *good* the ones who took a special interest in him. He graded a few as bad. But by far the longest list contained the names of those rated as *indifferent*. This man had hoped to make a real contribution which would help others who were also unemployed. He had a great shock when he discussed his list with others who had been making the same rounds and found that their ratings differed markedly from his. It became very obvious to him that the differences in agencies were, for the most part, differences in personal reactions. He never did complete his list. The best agency for one man may be the very worst for another, and so I must tell you reluctantly that you alone will have to decide which agency is the best one for you.

City versus Small-Town Agencies

Judging from the experiences of many individuals, there is quite a contrast in the methods of big-city and small-town employment agencies. The ones in large cities seem to be overwhelmingly busy with "bread and butter" jobs. These are the jobs for the masses of unemployed people—the office clerks, stenographers, business machine operators, etc. These people can be rather quickly processed and placed, and they are the backbone which provides the agencies with their main income.

A former president of the National Association of Employment Agencies said in *The Wall Street Journal:* "None of the group's members specializes in placing high-salaried men. Employment agencies find executive placement unprofitable because it takes so long to line up a middle-aged former boss with a job." In the same issue, a former controller says: "I tried the employment agencies and found that nobody wanted to talk to a 48-year-old man."

Men seem to have a much warmer feeling toward agencies outside the big metropolitan centers. Mr. W. H. wrote me, "I had four good interviews arranged for me by an employment agency in this small Connecticut manufacturing town. The job I took came as a result of one of these four leads."

Jobs can, and should, be obtained through agencies. Therefore, you should follow up all employment-agency advertisements that seem to be in your field. The people who run these agencies fill an economic function. They make possible the matching of people to jobs. Inasmuch as the bulk of these jobs is at the clerical level, don't expect too much of the agency. This is a letter I received not too long ago:

DEAR CARL,

You may recall that you asked me to send you some of the statistics of my long, hard, six months' job hunt. For some reason, I feel embarrassed about them, but here they are for what they are worth:

> I have had 137 "courtesy" interviews.
> I am listed with 17 employment agencies.
> I am registered with 29 recruiters.
> I answered over 75 newspaper ads—however, I attached a résumé and wrote the wrong kind of letter.

The job I landed came through answering an ad in *The New York Times*. I adapted my broadcast letter and did not enclose a résumé. The company had been searching for six months, and my letter just clicked with them.

Use recruiters and employment agencies but do not depend too much on them for that job. Keep the initiative for getting interviews in your own hands by getting out your broadcast letters. I consider the use of employment agencies a very passive way of pursuing a job. You would be depending on chance to lead you to openings. Agency openings shrivel and dry up during depression periods. Then again, the leads that come through agencies are not of the same quality as those you develop yourself. When you go from an agency to an interview, you have not had the opportunity to do your homework for that interview. You go in labeled as someone "looking for a job."

On the contrary, when you go in to an interview as a result of an invitation which has come from your letter, you go in with the cards stacked in your favor, for your letter has prepared the way.

My thirty years of experience in coaching job-seekers has taught me not to sell short *any* means of getting placed. I am a great believer in shaking every tree and turning over every stone. Nevertheless, it is foolish to spend too much time in panning streams where others have found pay dirt all too infrequently.

CHAPTER *10*

Life Can Begin for You at Fifty-or Sixty-or...

Time and again I have been told by people in their sixties and even in their fifties, "I am too old to be employable." Now and then I hear this from those who are only forty-five. This makes me boil, and I say to them in exasperation, It isn't your age that is against you—it is you yourself. You have been talking to the wrong people. Friends, employment agencies, and prospective employers have told you that if it weren't for your age they would be glad to consider you. Has it not occurred to you that being told that you are too old is one of the lamest and commonest excuses ever invented? This is what personnel people throw at you when at first glance, you do not meet their preconceived notion of the person they had in mind for a particular job. It is like trying for a role in a play, and the casting director may think he wants a tall man— but you are short. The casting director may, therefore, think

154

that you cannot play the part, no matter what your talents may be. Therefore, if you want to avoid the "Sorry, but" answer by the personnel manager, you should prepare him in advance to consider your talents first, and then weigh them against your other attributes. When an employer has no opening in his company, or if he has a preconceived idea of the type of person he wants, he may give you lame excuses which provide him with a sort of defensive facade.

Are Sex, Religion, Color, and Nationality Handicaps?

Actually, I have never found that any of these made any real difference. I have placed men and women, of every color, race, and religion, in good jobs. To be sure, there are always some employers to whom these doings *do* make a difference. It may very well be his employees who are prejudiced and they may have affected his decision. You may as well accept the fact that neither you nor anyone else in the world is going to be acceptable to *everyone*. This is a country of free choices.

In the chapter on "Developing Interview Leads Through Broadcast Letters," I stated that you could expect to get interviews from only about 6 per cent of your letters. Do you realize that this means that the oridinary job-hunter is *unacceptable* to ninety-four out of every one hundred prospective employers? Note that only six of the possible one hundred employers even asked the job-hunter to drop in for an interview, and these job-seekers were without any so-called handicaps. It is usually *you* yourself, because of some unfortunate past experience, who have developed a feeling of inferiority about race, sex, religion, or nationality. You are the person who considers them handicaps.

Turn Your Stumbling Blocks into Stepping Stones to Greater Opportunities

Some years ago I remember hearing the statement, "A man becomes enlightened and educated when he awakens to the fact that stumbling blocks can be turned into stepping stones." I do not remember who the author was, but that statement has made a lasting impression on me. It is the hardships of life that mold us; our handicaps become advantages, if we give them half a chance.

Jimmy Durante made a fortune from his extraordinarily large schnozzle. Did he ever cover up his nose when he went on stage? On the contrary, he never failed to call attention to it, and accentuated it even more with a long cigar. Myron Cohen, the great Jewish humorist, doesn't hide his religion; he uses it, and the public adores him for it.

Do you remember the story about Dr. George Washington Carver? As a frail young slave, he was traded for a broken-down horse. When this Negro was over seventy years old, Henry Ford asked him to come and work for the Ford Motor Company. He offered to set up a laboratory and supply him with ample research funds. He also offered him a salary as large as a king's ransom. Why did Ford do this? Was it out of pity, or was it the outgrowth of a charitable impulse? No, absolutely not, not the way I have read the story. Dr. Carver, working in his little laboratory at Tuskegee Institute, had discovered some uses for the lowly peanut and sweet potato. This completely changed the economy of the one-crop agriculture of the South. He went on to develop hundreds of new industrial and food products. Henry Ford wanted this man to go on finding even more uses and products, unhampered by lack of equipment and money. His underlying reason was that what was good for the South and good for agriculture would also be good for the Ford Motor Company. Mr. Ford says in his autobiography, "If I want the farmer to buy cars and tractors, I have to help him to make the money to do it. A farmer can get money only through what he produces. The more he produces and the more money he makes from his products, the easier it will be for him to buy my tractors."

Do not expect any business to be charitable. You, no matter what your handicaps, would not want to take advantage of them. You, as much as any other person in industry, have an obligation to help your company make a profit.

Be Objective

If you will think objectively about both yourself and about business, your job-getting battle is half won. Disregard completely your age, your sex, your color, your race and your religion and stop feeling sorry for yourself. You, in common with everyone else with a sincere purpose in life, have something to offer. It is your big job to present your past in such a way that it is acceptable. To accomplish this, wage a job campaign as though you had no handicaps. You may, however, have to send out many more letters than others do in order to give the law of averages a chance. It will work unfailingly on your side.

A Caution About Salary

How necessary is it that you must have as large a salary as you earned before you retired? Some people turn down a perfectly good salary, feeling that anything except what they got in their prime is beneath them. Is it not much better to get on the payroll and try to show how much you can contribute to the company's well-being? Don't forget that not too long ago you felt you were not wanted on account of your age. Now that someone has enough faith in you to give you a chance, might it not be up to you to show a little confidence in your employer?

The following are copies of letters sent out by people with so-called handicaps. They are included here to give you an example of the style to achieve, not to copy. You must be *yourself* or you will lose out in the interviews. Do not exaggerate. Tell the truth and nothing but the truth; otherwise your job will be short-lived.

How a Seventy-Five-Year-Old Man Got a Good Job

A seventy-five-year-oldster, Mr. C., was doing odd jobs as an accountant. He would set up a bookkeeping system and then go in once a week to make entries for small service companies. I knew this man because he had done just such a job for some of my friends. I had supposed that he was content with his varied but very small undertakings. I had no idea that he had aspirations to get into something that would give him more substantial earnings. One day he stopped me and said, "Mr. Boll, I see you help many people get jobs. Is there any help you can give me? I will gladly pay you for it." I assured him that I would see what I could do for him, but as for pay, that was out. I had never taken a penny from anyone for helping them, and I was not about to start now.

I got him to tell me about himself. As his story unfolded I became more and more interested. At one time he had his own public accounting firm, employing more than fifty auditors. He was a graduate of one of our best preparatory schools and also of an Ivy League college. I questioned him exhaustively about what he had done and asked him to try to dig up one thing from his memory that he was especially proud of.

Finally he said, "Yes, there is something of which I am especially proud—I designed and installed the accounting system for all the towns in Westchester County. This system was then copied by many of the other counties in the state, and it is still being used." Later on he continued, "It may interest you to know that I used to do the auditing for Sing Sing Prison." I asked him how many times he had been in the prison. "Twenty-six times" was the reply. I jumped at this and said, "Man, this is wonderful!" "I don't see anything wonderful about it," he said. "Yes," I replied, "This is truly wonderful; we can mention this in your opening sentence and say something like this—I have been in Sing Sing Prison a number of times." "Oh, really!" he said. "I couldn't possibly say that; I am a professional man; I am a certified public accountant. What would the profession think of me?" I persuaded him that the profession had not worried about his bad luck heretofore, and they were not likely to start now. I remember saying to him, "Let's try it. You are looking for a job and not a professional engagement." Thus, the following letter went out to several hundred New York corporations:

Mr. John Doe, President,
Products Company
—— Building
New York, N.Y.

DEAR MR. DOE:

I have been in Sing Sing Prison twenty-six times. Each was a professional visit as a public accountant to examine the accounts, costs, and management of the prison. That is but one type of my work.

Your company may need on its regular staff a man of seasoned experience to assume the accounting control. If so, you will undoubtedly be interested in my training and achievements.

I have done general audit work for governments, for nearly every kind of business enterprise, light and heavy industry, and public and private institutions. I have installed many systems of accounts, of financial and cost controls, trained personnel to operate them, and managed as treasurer or controller the accounts and finances of various corporations.

For the townships of Westchester County, New York, I designed and installed an accounting system that was recommended by the State Bureau of Municipal Accounts as a model for other townships of the state to follow. It has been widely copied and is still in use.

I have been office manager and supervising senior for some of the best-known accounting firms; have been a certified public accountant since 1916, have lectured on accounting at Columbia University and elsewhere; and have managed my own accounting business for over twenty years.

Accounting can be learned from books, but there is no substitute for experience. I can boast of a long period of active years in the profession.

I am draft-exempt, in perfect health, and am used to turning out two or three times as much work as younger men. I have prepared a more detailed résumé of my training and equipment which I would like to discuss with you with a view to serving your company in a productive capacity.

Very truly yours,

This letter was a fabulous success. Two weeks later, Mr. C. had accepted offers from two companies—one on a four-hour-a-day basis with a manufacturer of scientific equipment and the other with a maker of heavy machines. For this latter concern he became an internal auditor, working from 2 P.M. to

9 P.M. each evening. Just one month later he was promoted to take charge of all internal auditing. He then dropped his part-time job.

See how this letter has a "ho hum" opener. It is a topical opening sentence. Of course, an opening with such power is not always available. Notice how the second paragraph and the others follow the magic formula. Note also that this letter prepares the recipient for the fact that this man is mature. "I . . . have been a certified public accountant since 1916" and "I . . . have managed my own . . . business for over 20 years." "Accounting can be learned from books, but there is no substitute for experience. . . . I am draft-exempt . . . and am used to turning out two or three times as much work as younger men."

I am stressing these points: First, the man is using his so-called age handicap as an asset. Second, he is preparing the reader not to expect a young squirt. Third, if this man had come in in a wheel chair, or leaning on a cane, the interviewer would not have been shocked.

How a Russian Army Man Got a Good Job After Letters of Recommendation Failed

Alexander Igor G. had been a colonel in the Russian White Army. He told me that he and his group had held back the Russians in the Crimea until they could evacuate the thousands and thousands of people fleeing from the Bolsheviks. He himself was one of the last to get out. When he arrived in the United States he took a job shoveling coal for a huge boiler. His second job was a little better: he became a baker with one of the large biscuit companies. His third job was acting as an armed guard on an armored car which delivered valuables. By now he had earned enough money and had learned enough English to get into graduate business school. He was very eager to learn the American way of doing things. When he got out of school he got a job as financial editor of foreign securities. This job vanished in the early forties, and it was then that he came to see me. His case, even to me, seemed a tough one.

Here was a man nearly sixty, with a foreign accent, and foreign manners. I happened to mention this man's handicaps(?) to one of my neighbors, an officer in one of our large banks. This neighbor spoke Russian, for he was in Russia during World War I. He was most sympathetic and invited the Russian colonel to come to see him. During the visit he offered him five letters of introduction to friends who might be able to help. The colonel accepted the letters gratefully and started on the round of visits. When I next saw the colonel he told me that he had had an unbelievable experience. His five letters had produced many letters of introduction to others, and he had kept track of his calls. Altogether, he had received 150 letters of introduction, each passing him on to another. Every letter had been sympathetic and friendly, but not one of these letters had resulted in a job. This is the saga of letters of introduction; and I have seen it happen over and over again. They very seldom produce results. Often this has a demoralizing effect.

I persuaded Colonel G. to try the direct-mail approach, and, consequently, he mailed out the following letter to ten public accounting firms:

DEAR SIR:

In my recent job, I audited the financial statements and accounts of hundreds of organizations. I have probed in depth into their earning and pay-off ability.

Your organization may need someone of my experience and training for its auditing division. If so, you may be interested in what I have done.

I specialized in accounting at a school of business administration. I took every course they offered in accounting, industry, auditing, costs, budgeting, and statistical control.

As financial analyst, I wrote the financial reports which banks and investment companies used as a basis for making extended loans amounting to many millions of dollars.

Before attending the business school, I had received engineering and mathematical training in the Russian Army. I rose to the rank of colonel.

I will be happy to discuss with you the possibility of employment in your organization.

Yours truly,

I felt that we could have improved on the letter, but it worked, so we had no chance to write it over again. Three weeks later, Colonel G. was working as an auditor for one of our top-ranking accounting firms. He was putting in a full day's work, plus overtime, working from 9 A.M. to 9 P.M., also working Saturdays. Incidentally, one of the first audits he made was of the baking company where he had worked as a baker.

Note that in his letter he prepares the prospective employer for the fact that he is a Russian immigrant, or refugee, so that the employer will not be surprised when he sees him. There never was a more excited person than my Russian colonel when he called to tell me he had a position. Here is a paragraph from his letter to me:

May I express my feeling of gratitude and highest appreciation. Without your kind personal attitude toward me, your authoritative guidance to help me solve my difficult problem, I would probably still be idle.

Color Was No Bar to This Black

The following letter was mailed out by a younger man, a black:

DEAR SIR:

I am a recent graduate of ——— University where I majored in marketing. I have just completed my military service.

Your company may be looking for a man in your marketing division. If so, you may be interested in what I have done.

In my present job I have organized direct-mail campaigns for mailing up to 1,700,000 letters. I have done Market Research and Sales Forecasting.

I created a promotional gimmick which established sales distribution and gained label recognition for a previously unknown recording firm.

During my war service, I was program director of a Far East network on Okinawa.

I was graduated *cum laude* from ——— University where I was also a varsity letter man. I was the first black ever to receive the "Student of the Year" award.

I will be glad to discuss my education and business experience with you in a personal interview.

Very truly yours,

This is his report to me: "The results of my campaign were very successful. I mailed out 249 letters and received almost 50 per cent return in answers. Out of these, I had a total of 16 interviews—a 6.4 per cent interview rate. The interviews were very interesting and showed up several really good opportunities. The one with the ——— Company was so outstanding that I could not pass it up. My job is to organize the market for blacks. Eventually, I hope to be in charge of this end of the company's business for the whole United States. I just could not pass up this job."

How a Foreigner Who Had a Bad Leg Injury and a Speech Impediment Got a Good Job

I have mentioned before that there is always someone in the market place who wants to buy your special talents. All you have to do is to let enough people know about the "merchandise" that is available.

Recently, a young Pakistani national came to me for help. He had been having a very difficult time getting placed. He was a most remarkable person. He had been educated at Punjab University in Lahore. He graduated with top honors in international law. He had managed a 1,000-acre land development company and had carved a productive farm out of virgin land. He had been selected to be the leader of a farm exchange group to come to the United States. He had lived for a year with American farm families in the Middle West. He was an excellent speaker and had seventy-five times addressed different audiences, including the U.S. House of Representatives Agricultural Committee. He spoke English, Arabic, Urdu, Hindustani, and Punjabi. The year before he came to me he had been in a serious automobile accident. The accident had left him with a limp and a temporary speech impediment. Consequently, it was hard to understand him. In his letter campaign he paid absolutely no attention to his handicaps. Instead, he stressed his knowledge of the Middle and Near East. This is his letter:

DEAR SIR:

Recently, I graduated from the ——— Business School. I am a national of Pakistan. I am in the United States on a resident's visa, free to remain as long as I wish.

Your company may be interested in someone of my background to plan the marketing and selling of your products to countries of the Near East. If so, here are a few statements of my experience.

I read, write, and speak fluently the four major languages of the Near and Middle East—Arabic, Urdu, Hindustani, and Punjabi—in addition to fluent English.

The ways of life, customs, and laws of these lands are an integral part of my heritage and existence.

I organized and managed the placing of 1000 acres of land under cultivation. I also supervised one of the few large mechanized farms in Pakistan.

I graduated from Punjab University of Lahore with a major in International Law, where I ranked first in my class. I then practiced law in Pakistan.

I was elected leader of a delegation of Pakistani exchange students. After I came to this country, I lived for a year with several American families. I often spoke to different groups and made 75 speeches in all—one to the House Agricultural Committee of Congress, and one to the Rotary International Convention.

I shall be happy to discuss further my experience in respect to my being useful to you in your Asian market.

                                        Very truly yours,

He mailed out 112 letters. He received 76 replies, which resulted in ten interviews. He is now working for one of the nation's largest banks. Every single statement in the above letter gave direction to his specialty and knowledge of the East. He was a leader . . . a man who could be sent out to represent his company with stature in the foreign field.

Who, among you readers, would have traded places with

this man? He not only had a physical handicap but was of a religious and national minority.

You Are Never Too Old

Eric L. was sixty-two years old with a shock of white hair. When he came to me he stated flatly that he was unemployable. He had lost all his self-confidence and perspective. In his last job he had been making less than $10,000 so his wife had gone back to teaching school to help out. After I placed him in a new job he wrote, "I was positive that no employer really wanted me on account of my age and consequently I had little to look forward to. First, you persuaded me that my big trouble was lack of confidence; that if only I could get in to interview prospective employers there would be no difficulty in proving that my years and exeprience were assets. Second, you showed me that it was necessary that I prepare the employer in advance that I was no fledgling just out of school, so that when he caught sight of my pure white mane he wouldn't start looking for an excuse to terminate the interview." This is the paragraph wherein we solved the age problem: "I have spent thirty-two years in selling, from cold canvassing to sales management." Thus we turned his age handicap into an advantage. This did not affect the pulling power of his letter. Five hundred letters were mailed out and they brought in thirty requests for interviews. Here is his complete letter:

Mr. H. R. Johnson, President
——— Co.
——— Third Ave.
New York

DEAR MR. JOHNSON:

As manager of new business development of a firm selling intangibles, I increased business 80% in one year. To do this, I opened 14 new accounts totaling $100,000 in services to top executives. Among others, I developed and supervised sales training programs for three corporations, the largest in their field.

If your company needs someone in sales management, you may be interested in some of the other things I have done.

Previously, as Regional Sales Manager for a large firm selling intangibles to business executives, I built up the New England Region from the ground. My sales force led the entire country in average sales per man.

I opened an office at ———, Conn. to pioneer a District Manager plan, which was adopted nation-wide, and trebled sales volume in four years.

As a member of a departmental training staff, I recommended a new training policy which resulted in more than 50% reduction in the mortality of trainees.

I am a graduate of the ——— School and a member of the Sales Executives Club of New York. I have spent 32 years in selling from cold canvassing to sales management.

I will be glad to discuss further details of my experience in a personal interview.

> Very truly yours,

It was impossible for Eric L. to take all the interviews that were offered him, because when he had had half of them he received an offer which satisfied his requirements. He told me that each interview had helped to increase his confidence and his feeling of being of value to his employer.

Handicaps Never Keep You From Getting a Job

If you are a person with a handicap, I hope the experiences related in this chapter will inspire you, inspire you not to forget your handicap but to make an asset out of it. Never forget that in the market place there is a buyer for every product, but that buyer must be alerted to what is available. The job-getting techniques outlined in the previous chapters can be made to work for *everyone*. Use them and create your own future.

I received this thank-you letter only a month ago:

DEAR MR. BOLL:

I can't tell you how grateful I am that you wrote that book *Executive Jobs Unlimited*. Please thank your wife too for her "nagging."

I had polio when I was twelve years old and so I am slightly lame but I have always wanted to be in the business world. I have a magna cum laude from a women's college in Massachusetts and then went on for a M.B.A., also in Massachusetts.

I sold lingerie for two years in a large department store and then—a miracle—I found your book. I studied it and studied it and after working over my accomplishments for over a month, I sent out 30 broadcast letters. Yes, Mr. Boll, I remembered to say I was a bit lame. I got three interviews and am now assistant buyer of lingerie for a large department store. What a book!

God Bless,
Mary H. P.

CHAPTER *11*

For Women Only

"VIVE LA DIFFÉRENCE" shouted the French legislator as he jumped to his feet to reply to a colleague who had made some disparaging remarks about the opposite sex. Women have come a long way since that day. Now they are working and even fighting alongside men. Women's worldwide earnings in 1978 topped $400 billion. In comparison, men will earn $670 billion. Today many women are in fields and jobs formerly reserved for men. In the last decade there has been an increase of 11 per cent in the number of married women who work. More than half of all mothers with children under eighteen were in the working force in 1978. This is a higher ratio than in any previous group of working mothers, according to the Women's Bureau of the Labor Department. Opportunities for women have expanded enormously. It is now not only acceptable but fashionable for women to be employed.

After years of being overlooked, women are catching up in

all the professions. Though prejudice still exists, ability is beginning to outweigh gender in hiring and promotions. We now have many female economists, educators, doctors, aviators, and government workers. We have women in the Army, the Navy, and the Coast Guard. Many women are entering blue-collar fields and even more are advancing in business.

One of the nation's most effective economists is Alice Mitchell Revlin, the director of the Congressional Budget office which was created to give objective advice to Congressmen on the cost and effectiveness of various government programs, but even she says "Things are better now for women economists but history is hard to break. . . . The ranks are very thin in my age group." Juanita Krebs is the first economist as well as the first woman to become Secretary of Commerce. Nancy Hays Teeters has become the first woman member of the Federal Reserve Board.

In the field of education, women are also achieving important positions. The University of Chicago has named Dr. Hanna Holborn Gray as president. The first woman to head a major School of Business is Norma Loeser, who has been named Dean of the George Washington University School of Government and Business Administration.

Women are hardly new to the field of medicine but seldom have the top jobs gone to women. Recently, however, Dr. Mary Howell was named the first female dean of the Harvard Medical School, indicating that the wave of the future is coming closer.

Women are taking on great responsibilities in the aviation industry, both as pilots and as administrators. Mary Anderson was recently appointed Associate Administrator of the Federal Aviation Administration, the highest aviation post held by a woman as of 1978. Also in that year, Jill Brown, a black woman, qualified as a pilot for Texas International Airlines. Women are now in the space programs. In December, 1978, there were six women chosen by NASA to be astronauts in the Space Shuttle Program, and 1,500 more women applied for astronaut training.

The Army announced that Brigadier General Mary E. Clark, the last director of the WACS, is to become the first woman to command a major Army base when she is assigned to Fort McLellan, Alabama. The Army also reported that it will begin recruiting women from all the services for the honor guard detachments at the White House in response to "pressure from Rosalynn," who asked why there were no women in the honor guard.

For more than two hundred years the Navy has been dominated by men and now Navy Secretary W. Graham Claytor has approved a plan to assign women full time to fifty-five sea-going ships. On November 2, 1978, Mary Pat Carroll and several other Navy women reported for sea duty in Norfolk and in California. They were the first to take assignments on Navy vessels other than hospital ships or transports. They are also the vanguard of 56 women officers and 375 enlisted women who will help operate twenty-one noncombat ships in the Atlantic and Pacific fleets in the next few years. By 1984, the Navy hopes to have 5,130 female officers and enlisted women on ocean-going ships.

At Coast Guard commencement exercises, Brock Adams, Secretary of Transportation, said that women will soon serve aboard previously all-male Coast Guard cutters with long assignments at sea.

Women are even taking on tough blue-collar jobs that were formerly bastions of male employment. In 1978 the

Labor Department announced quotas for having blue-collar women on federal and federally related projects. This growing group of female workers is recognized in a recent Sears catalog that introduces a new line of women's work clothes "with heavy thread, rugged fabric, and heavy-duty pockets."

Women are on the rise everywhere but even more so in the business world. The number of female executives and directors is increasing rapidly. It will increase faster as more women gain confidence in their abilities. Almost all the large corporations now have at least one woman on their board. Today there are 296 women serving on boards whereas in 1969 there were only 46. The Equitable Assurance Society board has 4 women. Women who have become directors have been described as outspoken, provocative in their thinking, and as women of very outstanding achievement.

In a survey of some of these women, they were asked what contributed most to their success. In addition to "hard work and sacrifice" most of them mentioned "luck."

Men always seem to have an "ole boy" or a buddy system that reduces their need for luck in the business world, while women are more likely to be isolated in their jobs. Women are beginning to solve this problem, not by laying siege to locker rooms or male breakfast clubs but by forming their own organizations that will make the buddy system work for them. They can then get to know each other personally, in addition to exchanging job information. Now there are a good many organizations where women can get help. Elinor Guggenheim was responsible for the organizing of the New York Forum, which now has 155 members. Barbara Walters, Carol Bellamy, Shana Alexander, Bella Abzug, and Bess Myerson are all members. Women must excel in their field in order to join this group. There are groups like this in other cities. In San Francisco there is the Professional Woman's Alliance; in Pittsburgh there is the Executive Women's Council; in Philadelphia it is called the Forum of Executive Women. These groups are now trying to band together to form a national forum and this summer the representatives from New York, Colorado, and North Carolina are meeting to decide on criteria for a national board.

The New York City Y.W.C.A. has recently formed the Academy of Women Achievers. They found in their survey that half of the women were from forty-six to fifty-five years old. Half had completed some graduate work or had advanced degrees. Sixty per cent of them said that "on the job" training had been more helpful to them than anything else. Forty-one per cent of them acknowledged that they earned more than their husbands but that the wage gap was no problem. Eleven per cent had salaries between $16,000 and $30,000, 32 per cent earned between $31,000 and $50,000, 18 per cent made $75,000 to $100,000, and 7 per cent earned more than $100,000 a year. When asked what advice they would give women on the way up, they stressed the fact that to get ahead a woman must plan for the next step, work hard and long, and not shirk responsibility. They must be assertive but not aggressive.

Another great help for women is a non-profit organization started by Felice Schwartz called Catalyst. For seventeen years, it has been helping women choose, launch, and advance their careers. It offers counseling through a national network of women's resource centers. In addition to helping women launch their careers, Catalyst is committed to working with the business community. In her letter to me, Jeanine Green, the vice-president, says, "Corporations have expressed time and time again to us the difficulty of finding qualified women for managerial and executive positions." The real problem, she says, is that women are unsure about searching for the top positions, or how to present their credentials. The annual report observes, "In view of the fact that 72 per cent of career opportunities are in business and industry, it is imperative that women be encouraged to understand that business and industry offer creative, challenging rewarding jobs of an immense variety." Their Corporate Board Resource has on file the dossiers of 746 top-level women candidates, for corporations searching for women board members.

Another Catalyst service is directed at women currently serving on corporate boards. A symposium of women directors of Fortune's 1,300 companies is being held this year. Here the women can discuss topics pertaining to board service. Of these 1,300 companies with 17,000 director's positions, only 296 are held by women.

The Catalyst Information Center in this last year has answered 18,000 inquiries. For further information, contact National Headquarters, Catalyst, 14 East 60th Street, New York, New York 10022; 212-759-9700.

Your First Job

In order to get on the payroll of a company, a bank, an advertising agency, a publishing house, a non-profit organization, or any other business, you must have a starting position. Many have gained a foothold by graduating from special schools or getting M.B.A.'s from business schools. Others get into the flow by starting as secretaries, bookkeepers, stenographers, or cashiers.

Whatever your starting position, be sure that once you are established, you start preparing yourself for the next higher job. When you have thoroughly mastered your present job, look for opportunities for expanding. Work overtime occasionally, volunteer extra work when someone is ill or on vacation. Think of ways to improve things and when the time seems right, discuss your ideas with your superior. At the same time, discuss your job with her so she can help you formulate meaningful goals. She will be delighted to do this, for whatever progress you make, makes her look better too. Ask her if there are certain courses that would be helpful to you in your job or whether she can suggest any reading material for you that would be helpful. Your boss will rightly gather from all this that you are ambitious and are taking your work seriously. Then, when there is an opening higher up and you feel you have developed the necessary skills to handle it, ask to be considered for the job. Do NOT expect that it will be handed to you. ASK for it.

If you cannot get a better job in your present company, there are plenty of others who will need you. You will simply have to go through the same job-getting procedures described in the rest of the book. This means the route of résumés and broadcast letters.

The Résumé

Your résumé should be a complete list of your accomplishments and skills. It is from this list that you pick out the outstanding ones for your broadcast letter. Many women will say at this point, "I don't have the kind of accomplishments I can write about." Forget it. Everyone can list accomplishments if they try hard enough. Even the woman who hasn't yet worked for pay has accomplishments to report. Sit down, start a list, put it aside for a few days, and you will find that you can add to it as you recall certain incidents. Take your time and you will gradually have a good list. Now try to put in measurements for what you have done. For instance, if you are a housewife, tell how much you saved by purchasing children's clothing at sales and at certain times of the year. If you have done volunteer work, report how many hours you worked, how many people you helped, and so on. Tell exactly what responsibilities you carried. Remember, as Henry Ford once said, "You can't build a reputation on what you are going to do, but on what you have done."

Once you have a starting position, be sure to keep track of how you have improved results so you can include these statistics in the résumé you use for getting your next position. If you want a better position in retailing, for instance, keep track of how you have increased turnover, increased profits, reduced costs. Find out what the volume of business was before you came into the picture, and by what percentage you increased it. Determine whether you accomplished this with the same amount of capital invested in inventory. These figures may seem small and unimpressive to you, but when you give them to your superior or to your future boss they become quite meaningful. They help you to stand out as one who has a positive impact on retailing. Reread Chapter 2 for further information on composing résumés.

The Broadcast Letter

Though résumés sometimes serve a purpose, I recommend using them sparingly. In my experience, broadcast letters are far more effective. Résumés are so often tossed into the wastebasket. I like to refer to their mailing as the "kiss of death." I know a woman who had been requested four times to mail in a résumé. Each time she mailed instead her first broadcast letter. Finally she was invited to Boston with her expenses paid. She got the best paying job she has ever had.

You should use the broadcast letter as bait in order to get interviews. This letter must not dwell on the hopes you have for getting the job but only on things you have accomplished. Use paragraphs from your résumé to compose your broadcast letter. If you are applying for specific kinds of jobs, use only those paragraphs that have to do with that particular job.

These letters must be short and concise and direct the reader to the kind of job you want. They must give some measurement of what you have accomplished in that particular field. Remember, a list of functions alone is like "salt without savor." It is the numerical recital of figures with your performances that makes you the outstanding woman—that one in a hundred. Here is a letter which shows that this procedure is applicable to ANY kind of job. This young friend of mine desperately wanted a teaching position in spite of the fact that there is a surplus of teachers wanting jobs. The letter netted her six interviews and the job.

I am a 1975 graduate of Bay Path Junior College with a degree in Child Study. My curriculum included one year practice teaching a class of 16 four-year-old children.

If you are looking for a nursery school or prekindergarten teacher, you may be interested in some additional details of my experience.

I was entrusted with the care and feeding and transportation of a boy and girl (12 and 10 years old) intermittently over a two-year period as a "Mother's Helper" for a working mother.

Previously, as manager of a refreshment stand for a 500 family country club, I was personally accountable for sales receipts in excess of $100 per day.

I was also responsible for maintaining an inventory record of more than 50 items and ordering replenishment stock weekly.

As a telephone solicitor for a daily newspaper I have averaged over 5 subscriptions per day during college vacations for the past year.

I have my Red Cross Senior Life Saving and Water Safety Instructor certificate.

I will be happy to discuss your needs and additional relevant details of my experience, including personal references, with you in a personal interview.

Very truly yours,
Margaret T.

Here is another good broadcast letter that worked.

If your company is in need of a marketing manager, you may be interested in what I have accomplished.

As marketing manager of a consumer products company

—I initiated a design change which helped raise production by 25%. This lifted my division's sales beyond the $5,000,000 mark.

—I made a design suggestion which corrected a fault. This saved thousands of dollars and eliminated former complaints.

—I set up a new sales organization which by my inspiration and management increased sales from 80 to 100%.

—I standardized the construction of some of our products.

—I suggested innovations in our products and this broadened our scope, thus making it possible for us to enter two new markets.

I have an M.B.A. from New York State University and also an undergraduate degree in mechanical engineering.

I shall be happy to discuss any employment possibilities with you in a personal interview.

Yours truly,
Janet P.

The following broadcast letter also led to a job for the writer:

Mr. John Jones, President
Hanover Prestigue Merchandise, Inc.
New York, New York

DEAR MR. JONES:

As a buyer for the women's ready-to-wear department in a well-known store, I increased the sales volume from $250,000 to $500,000 a year. This increased the profits by 25%. As the only woman buyer, I developed the sale of higher margined exclusive merchandise.

If your organization is in need of someone for your specialty ready-to-wear department, you might be interested in what I have done.

—Made the store known for its exclusive selections.

—Provided a higher markup and profit margin each season.

—Got a Swiss fabric manufacturer to sell our store selected patterns for our exclusive use.

—Persuaded and made agreements with two manufacturers to produce certain specified styles for our store only. We furnished the fabrics.

I am a graduate of a well-known designer's school. I shall be glad to discuss my experience with you in a personal interview.

Yours truly,
Shirley S.

Address
Telephone number

The Interview

If you have written good broadcast letters, you will have appointments for your first interviews. Be calm and do not panic. There is a job waiting for you around the corner. It is the unknown present that causes your flutters. You will eventually look back on interviews as exhilarating experiences. Take all the interviews you can get.

Dress for an interview in an attractive suit or a pants suit. Very high heeled shoes, too tight a sweater, too flamboyant a hairdo, have no place in an office. Do not try to be unusual in your manner of dress. You will do better to appear dependable and agreeable.

Do not use your femininity as a way to get attention from men. There is a vast difference in the way men treat women in an office and in the social world. Remember, you are here to do a job and not to call attention to yourself as a woman.

Before you go into your first interview, be prepared. Please reread the chapter in this book on "How to Conduct an Interview." Many people have written to me saying that this was the most valuable advice in their job campaign.

Take every interview you can get even though the job may not be quite what you are looking for. Practice will sharpen your interviewing technique and give you ease in handling it.

Go in with at least five pertinent questions in a small loose-leaf notebook, questions that show that you have researched the company, questions that reveal that you are aware of the fact that the company must make a profit or it will cease to exist.

Do NOT ask questions about salary, working time, length of vacations and coffee breaks. Such self-serving questions may be of importance to you, but nothing will turn the interviewer off faster. Ask instead questions about the job requirements.

You will learn to keep control of most interviews by asking questions. Remember that most interviewers know as little about interviewing as you do and are just as hesitant about the situation as you are. So you make it easier for them by asking questions about their products, about other companies doing the same things, etc. Keep throwing the ball to the interviewer.

Avoid an interview over the telephone. Just say, "It is impossible for me to talk to you right now. I'll drop in to see you. Will Tuesday be all right or shall I try Wednesday or Thursday?"

Never say that salary is unimportant, even though it is. Never mention that you have independent means. Even when you do get to discussing salary, keep your other sources of income out of the discussion. Employers want hungry people.

Some interviewers take advantage of unknowledgeable women by asking questions that are unallowable.

The Human Rights Division of New York State has made it known that there are definite rulings on questions that may be asked of applicants. Last year the State Legislature amended the Human Rights Law to make it illegal for interviewers to ask dozens of personal questions commonly asked in the past. They point out that it is illegal for a prospective employer or landlord to inquire about marital status, either directly or indirectly through such questions as "Do you want to be addressed as Miss or Mrs.?" There are other blanket prohibitions such as questions about birth control or future plans for having children. They may not ask the applicant's place of birth, whether the applicant is a native-born or naturalized American citizen, national background, or religion. Neither may they ask an applicant to "list all clubs and societies to which you belong." They cannot require or even suggest that the applicant enclose a photograph.

Below are listed some legal and illegal questions an interviewer might ask about age, arrest record, and health.

AGE. Legal question: Are you between eighteen and sixty-five years of age? If not, state your age.

Illegal question: "How old are you?" or "What is your date of birth?"

ARREST RECORD. Legal question: "Have you ever been convicted of a crime? Give details."

Illegal question: "Have you ever been arrested?"

HEALTH. Legal question: "Do you have any impairments that would interfere with your ability to perform the job for which you have applied?"

Illegal question: "Do you have a disability?" or "Have you ever been treated for any of the following diseases . . . ?"

The penalties for illegal inquiries range from a reprimand to a $500 fine. The Human Rights Commissioner urges anyone who has been asked an illegal question to file a complaint.

If you are asked any of the illegal questions, simply say very calmly, "I don't believe that question is allowable."

Women in the Changing World of Business

What new attitudes don't change, laws do. Forty states and the federal government prohibit sex discrimination in employment. Thirty-seven states and the federal government ban sex discrimination in pay.

Go into your job expecting equal treatment and you will be much more likely to get it. People usually treat you in the manner in which you expect to be treated.

Many employers contend that one of their biggest problems is in convincing women to take advantage of the Equal Rights Employment laws and the opportunities that they are offering. Women have for years been conditioned not to try *too* hard, so it is often difficult to convince them to try for a higher position.

Another hazard for women is in correctly handling sexual harassment. In a survey by a national magazine in response to a questionnaire answered by 9,000 women, 90 per cent of them admitted that they had been harassed. The Working Women's United Institute is one of several groups formed to help women who are facing this problem. As more women become aware of the fact that there is help, they are becoming more willing to talk about it. The W.W.U.I. is preparing a handbook to give these women moral support. Very few companies have a procedure for registering complaints, but in April 1979 the New York State Senate Minority Task Force on Women's Issues proposed legislation that would permit workers to collect unemployment compensation if they can prove that they had quit their jobs on account of sexual or verbal harassment.

Sexual harassment can start in many subtle ways. The first step in stopping it is to react immediately. If you do not stop the advances at once, they will get worse. If they do get worse, go right to the supervisor. When a woman feels her job is in jeopardy if she doesn't cooperate, she is being harassed. This is very different from an innocent flirtation or an affair between two equals. These unwanted advances destroy a woman's confidence in her ability. If they persist, there is always Title VII of the Civil Rights Act of 1964. She might, if she is fired, take the company to court. This is, however, a very last resort since it is expensive and the emotional pressure can be enormous. If this becomes public knowledge, it may prove to be a handicap in getting the next job.

Some women executives have a problem about delegating authority. The president of one of New York's top companies says that this is the single most difficult mistake that he sees women make. Most women have been used to doing things themselves if they want them well done. They are anxious about trusting subordinates with any real responsibility, so they allow their desks to be piled high, take all the telephone calls, try to type their own letters—and finally they are completely bogged down with petty details. Do not allow yourself to fall into this trap.

Every office has pockets of politics and intrigues. The most important piece of advice I can give you is that you stay aloof from them. Also stay away from the gossips. Neither should you allow yourself to be drawn into a clique. If pressed too hard simply say, "I am new here and want very much to consider you and everyone else here a friend." Do not get involved with those who make disparaging remarks about your bosses or about the company. If you do have opinions about them, keep them to yourself.

Finally, even though opportunities are getting better for women, do not expect favored treatment in your office because of your sex. The bottom line in business is PROFITS. Profits are sexless.

CHAPTER *12*

When You Are Back on the Payroll

YOU GOT BACK ON THE PAYROLL by telescoping all your talents and selling your new employer on the fact that you were the *one person in a hundred*, or even in a thousand, that he needed. Now you have an extraordinary chance to prove to him that he made no mistake in judgment.

Profit From Your Past Experience

How often in life have you wished that you could start all over again with a clean slate? Well, here is your chance. If you have made mistakes in the past, are you going to be honest enough with yourself to admit them? Are you going to try to avoid the same pitfalls in the future? Let's admit that your previous boss was wrong. While some of your co-workers cheered you on, you really told him off. Right or wrong, your former boss is still there on the job. Your fellow workers are also there, but you got bounced—there was not enough room for both you and the boss. You cannot afford to show up your boss. Neither can you afford to make him look small before his employees.

Perhaps you took sides in an office political battle. The slate is now clean, but have you resolved never again to get involved in anything of that nature? Some fourteen of the top echelon of the Curtis Publishing Company recently complained about the president to the Board of Directors. Most of the fourteen are gone, but the president is still there. Every human being could cite instances where he thought he had been treated unjustly. Harry Emerson Fosdick tells us that though the Bible promises many things, nowhere does it promise that we will be dealt with justly. Stop thinking about past mistreatments. Don't be an injustice collector, if you want to be a happy man. Remember: "Never chew your pills —swallow them. When you chew them, it makes them taste still more bitter."

This doesn't mean that you should stay aloof, be a prude, or be a loner. On the contrary, you should make friends among your associates and go out to lunch with them now and then. Sometimes include those above you, for you can learn much from them. They will give you greater insight into the whole business operation.

Be Modest

Don't let the president introduce you to your new associates as a superman or near genius. I know of a man who was introduced in just that manner. It proved to be an insurmountable barrier between his fellow executives and him. Be modest and friendly, but be very wary about mentioning your schools, your social and golf clubs, etc. Don't throw your weight around or tell anyone how good you are. If you are good, it will be known soon enough.

Your Long-Range Objective

What do you expect to be doing ten years from now? This is the time to assume a long-range objective. Set it high enough and then focus all your endeavors toward that goal. This will mean that both you and your family may have to make sacrifices. Be sure to talk this over with your family so that they will be understanding about your longer working hours, and your having to attend conventions and conferences. Make the decision now that you want to be one of the top people in your field. At the same time, plan that you will be picked for that top job and will not go seeking it. Any time you are offered a job from the outside—whether you take it or not—your prestige will have been enhanced.

Prepare For That Next Job

Keep preparing yourself for that next job, whether it be with your present company or with another. However, if you should find that you have made a mistake in joining a new company, do not prolong the error. Get out as soon as it is economically possible. You can't make a peach out of a lemon. When you are in an established position, the one thing you should do, in addition to doing a good job, is to set up a financial reserve. This might be in the form of savings accounts, bonds, or life insurance. Getting another job may take from one to six months. Build this reserve up conscientiously month by month. Do this and you release yourself from the fear of making a change.

The job-getting techniques which you learned in this book can be put to work for you over and over again. In your last campaign, if you had a difficult time getting your saleable merchandise together, i.e., your accomplishments, and your concrete "for instances," you can make it easier in the future.

Keep a notebook or diary about your business activity. Review and record, at least once a month, some report, study, or suggestion for which you can claim credit. Put down figures so you will have a measure of your achievements. Put them down even though you think of them as being insignificant. Some future employer may think otherwise.

Profit is the ultimate goal of every business. It is the basis on which the president of your company is judged. It will be the basis on which you, too, will be judged. If your measurable results reflect this theme, you are well prepared for the next job campaign.

Project Your Image

If the company you are joining has a public-relations department, get them to prepare a release for the newspapers. This should include your picture, your new title, the name of the company, and the name of its product. You will be amazed that almost the day following the press release, you will hear from recruiters, offering you their services should you need assistance, etc. You will also be told that your release has been placed in their permanent file, which means that sometime they may call you to fill a position.

If your new company does not have a public-relations department, you may find it a bit more difficult to get any publicity. In this case, you might suggest that the company is losing chances for valuable advertising, that periodic information should be released about the company and its officers (and incidentally about you).

Merely keeping your nose to the grindstone and being engrossed in your work will not guarantee your advancement. You must at the same time build recognition for yourself. This will not only benefit your company but will make you more attractive to recruiters and competitors. There are many ways to do this. One of the best ways is to accept every opportunity to read a paper or give a speech about your specialty before any group that makes such a request. Make certain that your boss has been asked to give his permission. He will be complimented and will have no reason to feel that you are a "publicity hound." Get reprints of your speech made so you can distribute them where it counts. Keep in mind that most people do not go to the bother of doing these things through sheer inertia. Your efforts here may be worth thousands of dollars to you.

Another good way to project your image is to write articles for publication. Your trade or association magazines are hungry for articles. Write about any interesting incident that has happened in connection with your specialty. Show it to the editors. If they are interested, have them get permission from your boss to print the article.

Conferences and Meetings

Many executives attend conference after conference without any advance preparation. Sometimes even the chairman has laid no foundation for the meeting. If you know what is going to be discussed, do a little advance thinking about the matter. Have a memorandum ready showing that you have your ideas well in hand. You will benefit both yourself and your company by your preparation.

Do not monopolize the meeting. Try to keep your remarks confined to only one of the subjects discussed. Do not try to force your ideas, and show no irritation if your ideas are not adopted. Ask one or two questions at every meeting, trying with each question to bring out a point for discussion. If the meeting went unusually well, don't hesitate to compliment the chairman.

Assume Responsibility

Be willing and ready to assume responsibility whenever you can, for most people shun it. If a special problem needs to be studied and reported on, volunteer to take it over. You may delegate some of the work to others, but you are the one who must pull the reports together, write the conclusions, and deliver them at the next meeting. If the boss wants the report sooner than that, get it to him. Have a copy made for each person it concerns and sign your name to your handiwork.

Often at a meeting, no one wants to be the conference secretary. Here is another chance for you to take on a job that no one wants. Draw up the notes and review the accomplishments of the meeting. Your secretary can do the work, but you should sign your name to the report.

Association Work and Public Speaking

Get into association work with your own professional organization—there are different ones for each field, i.e., controllers, sales managers, corporate secretaries, and purchasing agents. Take on committee work. Remember, it is always the busy man who can do more.

If you volunteer to serve on minor committees and do more than the minimum amount of work, you will probably be asked to be on the executive committee. Sooner or later you will be prevailed on to talk about the organization or about some part of it that is in your field. Few executives are willing, or able, to speak in public. Many of them will turn down all such requests—but not you. When it is discovered that you are willing to speak, you will have many opportunities to do so. Take every one of them, for there is nothing that will give you more credit and recognition than making a speech in public. You may gradually become a spokesperson for the industry before government authorities and legislative committees. See that your name is always connected with that of your company; after all, you are doing this on company time.

The formula for success used to be: "Learn your job, stick to it, work hard, and you will get to the top." In these days of fierce competition, this is no longer all that is necessary. In order for other people to find out about you, you must have the ability to communicate your ideas.

Public speaking will come very hard at first, but you can develop competency in this gradually. At first, you may even have to write in advance the questions you plan to ask in meetings. Then, step by step, you will find that it gets easier as you meet with one success after another, until you are finally ready to progress from giving a short report to making a brief speech. You are now on your way. It takes both effort and application to be that *one person in a hundred*.

Prepare For Promotion

All too frequently executives are fearful of training an assistant to be strong enough to take over. Don't adopt that attitude. If you are an executive, you should make your assistant so strong that he or she will push you right up the ladder. The development of executive leaders should be one of your conscious objectives. The most effective way of bringing out executive ability in others is to give them more and more responsibility. There is no surer way to ferret out competence. You must, of course, recognize that a person who makes decisions will also make mistakes. However, if your assistant makes the same mistake too often, it would suggest that you are giving him or her too much responsibility. Try to get your assistant, in turn, to pass responsibility on down to the next echelon. It will not be long before your division or section will be outstanding. Give praise where it is deserved and correction where necessary. General Patton is supposed to have said, "All men need a pat on the back once in a while; some need it high and some need it low." In teaching someone to replace you, you will be doing as much for yourself as you will do for him or her, for you must clarify your own responsibility and authority in the company. This will force you to achieve an understanding of the interdependence of your sector and the rest of the organization.

When You Are Offered Another Job

When you are offered another job, you will be forced to make a difficult decision. Some of the questions you will have to ask yourself are:

1. Does this job further my long-range objective? Don't let yourself be hypnotized into thinking you will necessarily be broadening your experience. Is someone painting the mirage of a greener pasture? This may be just another way station that lengthens the road to your ultimate goal.

2. Will the extra salary compensate you for switching from the known to the unknown?

3. Is someone offering you more money so that he can pick your brain and then throw you out? Are you being hired to do a very special "dirty" job that your new boss hasn't the guts to do himself? This might be closing a plant, moving a plant out of a community, or weeding out old employees on account of a merger. If you are being hired for this sort of "piece-work," find out what place there is for you in the organization when your project is completed.

4. Have you been offered a job in a family-owned business and been told that the boss (owner) is over sixty or seventy and wants to retire? He wants you to be trained to take over. Investigate this sort of situation very carefully. Try to find out whether others before you had been promised the same opportunity and had quit in frustration some time later. Consider carefully whether or not you will actually get the chance to take over. Too often the owner of a family concern won't let go his hold, even though he says he will. He considers the business his baby and he refuses to have it weaned. Insist upon a definite time for the take-over or turn down the job.

5. Are you taking another job because you want to get away from internal politics and squabbles? Have you ever heard of an organization that wasn't steeped in them?

6. Are you changing positions because you feel that your present boss is not giving you enough responsibility, that he is hanging on to you so that you won't get promoted out from

under him? How do you know that the next boss is going to
be more amenable?

7. Do you feel that you are a galley slave and want to get rid
   of your chains? Consider that your next set of chains may be
   shorter and heavier.

Weigh carefully the cause of your dissatisfaction—it might
be within yourself. It might be because of your approach to
the job and to your fellow workers.

When you do move to another job, do it with your eyes
wide open. Be sure it is a step toward your long-range goal.
Try to get a title, even though it may be only that of an
assistant to the controller, sales manager, or manufacturing
manager. Get your reponsibilities and duties outlined. Find
out what authority you are going to have to do the job. If
you are being taken in to succeed someone else after a period
of time, find out whether he or she has been told about this
and if that person is agreeable to having you as an understudy.
If not, you may find yourself the fifth wheel on the wagon.

Belong to the Team

You cannot be a "loner" in an organization. Belong to the
group, but avoid total commitment. Do not get so involved
that you lose the ability to think independently. Keep asking
yourself why a thing is being done a certain way and whether
there might not be a more economical and efficient method.
Do not ask your superiors these questions, for they may resent them. Opposition to your doing anything a new way will
come from two groups: (1) those who will fight new ideas
unless they originate them, and (2) the status quo preservers
who dislike the bother of doing anything different. The first

group will be more amenable to change if they are led to think that they originated the idea. You can do this by asking questions such as, "What would you think about trying to do it this way?"

Stimulate your assistants to think by subjecting them to questions such as, "Why are we doing it this way?" This will activate them into doing things a better way. Your department can ultimately become an outstanding example of cohesion and profitability, thus paving the way for your advancement.

Be Enthusiastic—Success Is Yours

Think and work for success and you will win it. Associate yourself with the optimists. Shun those who are always finding fault and blaming others for their own shortcomings. Exposing yourself to the enthusiasts will help you to remain enthusiastic. People like to be with people who exude confidence and who see the good side of life. Marshal Foch once said, "How is it that an army of 90,000 men can defeat an army of 90,000 men? The difference is that one of them believes in victory."

Job Security

I would like to think that there is such a thing as job security—so many people strive for it. The search for security has been more important than ever to men since the Great Depression. This attitude has affected the younger generation, who have no doubt been influenced by their teachers and their elders.

There is no such thing as *job security*. Time and again I

have noted well-known companies being merged or even liquidated. Their employees who thought of themselves as "sitting pretty" found themselves among the unemployed.

No one should worry about the security of his job. A desire for security, somehow, turns out to be one of the great inhibitors which keep you from standing up to your full height. It makes for "yes" men who dare not make decisions for fear of being wrong. Your full growth potential comes from making decisions, both right and wrong ones—particularly wrong ones. An intelligent person learns from mistakes. They contribute to growth. Do not hesitate to make decisions. Remember: the live trout always swims upstream, it's only the dead one that floats with the current.

There is no such thing as perfect security. A new process, a different technique, a substitute, cheaper labor, newer imports, etc., will close up companies even a hundred or more years old. There is no security in either government or military jobs. Whole sections or bureaus can be lopped off or abolished overnight.

Your only security is in yourself. You create it through your own attitudes and abilities. You create your own security by making and keeping yourself a wanted commodity. If you do this, you need never worry about security. There will always be a job. There are many jobs. There are better jobs.